There are some truths only poe[...]
that only poetry can reach. Chr[...]
this excellent poetry that it can[...]
and dislocation and offer healing words and liberating truth. Seamus
Heaney once said that the best poetry offers us "phrases that feed the
soul": this collection is full of excellent "soul food."
—Malcolm Guite
Priest, Poet

Chris Maxwell is the only person in my book who pens poetry I want
to sip, slurp, and guzzle; then pour another glass by turning to the
next page!
—Michele Pillar
GRAMMY nominated singer, speaker and author of the book, Un-
tangled, The Truth Will Set You Free

With this second volume of poetry, Chris Maxwell has found a new
rhythm. The words flow more confidently, more boldly, while the
voice is less restrained, less tentative. Chris has gained greater fluency
in poetic language, and it now seems like his native tongue. Emo-
tions, ideas, experiences, encounters, seasons, scenes—he captures
their essence and distills them into concentrated poetic form. An-
other beautiful book.
—Russell Board
Regional Director for Continental Asia
IPHC World Missions Ministries

There is surely a part of us that knows and understands that heal-
ing often involves discomfort and endurance. We nod our heads
and agree that it might need to get worse before it gets better. But,
honestly, nobody really likes that program very much. And that
knowledge doesn't seem to help us very much when we're right in
the middle of it all. In *embracing now*, Chris Maxwell shares personal
stories that make us feel less alone in our weaknesses. He creatively
describes things that are, by definition, hard to name, and encour-
ages us to keep faith even when unbelief might seem like the easy

way out. As you get to know how he thinks and feels, poem by poem and page by page, you may find yourself wishing you could sit across the table from this interior tour guide to talk it through. Unless and until that happens, this extended letter from a friend-not-yet-met will have to do!
— **Bob Bennett**
Singer-Songwriter

Chris Maxwell's second book of poetry, *embracing now*, is just what the doctor ordered if you are struggling to connect the dots of your faith with the contours of life this side of Eden! Continuing in the tradition of Chris's former writings, *embracing now* draws upon the life experiences, musings, lessons, devotional inspirations, and daily interactions covering the entire gamut of emotions. Rich in theological truth, Chris openly and intimately shares his questions, emotions, insights, and nuggets of wisdom learned in the heat of the battles of life itself. I thought his last book was his best, but Chris simply continues to astound with his command of language, nuance, cleverness, and brilliant imagination. I found myself engaging with each poem at a variety of different levels ranging from tears, laughter, smiles, head nods, and simply shaking my head in amazement at the profound gift of exquisite communication God has placed inside Chris. To the extent you allow yourself to enter the journey with him, you will receive more than you bargained for in this collection. Simply amazing!
—**C. Tracy Reynolds**
VP for Student Development
Emmanuel College

Chris Maxwell has done it again. Poetry that arrests, that stops us in our tracks, that makes us think and wonder, makes us weep, makes us smile. I love Jesus and a platform: ". . .and all tribes seemed to merge: when have tax collectors, priests, teachers, prostitutes, and children all mingled beside military might waiting for the sight of One claiming to be a Savior?" Chris makes us think about Jesus and his character—not bending to godless culture. Jesus and his methods—never exploitive or self-serving. Jesus and his love—always up close and personal. "Jesus, surprising the culture, was walking away. . .but a lonely lady finally felt loved for the first time in her life." So good. Thanks, Chris.

—Ron White, Ed.D.
President, Emmanuel College

embracing now: pain, joy, healing, living is an appropriate title for health. There is good pain and there's bad pain. Some forms of pain are part of the journey to death. Other forms of pain are pathways to life. Chris Maxwell takes us on this journey through stages of life, everyday experiences, and insights into the Bible. Poetry is not fluff reading. It's an invitation to reflection, thought, meditation. This collection will help you heal.

—Dr. Doug Beacham
General Superintendent
International Pentecostal Holiness Church

Chris Maxwell's second collection of poems, *embracing now: pain, joy, healing, living* continues Chris's honest meditations on the trials of being simultaneously both a caregiver and a sufferer of viral encephalitis and, beyond all of that, a man living an everyday life. His honesty about his trials throughout lends sincerity to his affirmations of belief and ultimate embrace of hope. Rather than producing a collection of predictable pieties, Chris works in the tradition of the psalmists, whose honest feelings permeated their ancient poetry alongside their very real doubts and their ultimate expressions of faith. As before, Chris's poetry is highly accessible to those unused to reading poetry but still engaging for those who read it regularly. Everyone who has ever lived and struggled, meaning everyone, can find something in these poems that will bring hope to their everyday lives.

—Dr. James Rovira
Multigenre/multimodal freelance writer, scholar, and poet

embracing now

pain, joy, healing, living

chris maxwell

True Potential
REACH THE WORLD

embracing now
pain, joy, healing, living
a collection of poems by chris maxwell

poem 4. "in the middle of your hurry" first appeared in *Pause for Moms: Finding Rest in a Too Busy World*, Chris Maxwell (True Potential: Travelers Rest, SC, 2013, page 189).

poem 8. "a song" first appeared in *Pause for Moms: Finding Rest in a Too Busy World*, Chris Maxwell (True Potential: Travelers Rest, SC, 2013, pages 305–306).

poem 9. "time flies when you're having sons" first appeared in *Pause for Moms: Finding Rest in a Too Busy World*, Chris Maxwell (True Potential: Travelers Rest, SC, 2013, pages 348–349).

poem 10. "the dying" first appeared in *Pause with Jesus: Encountering His Story in Everyday Life*, Chris Maxwell (True Potential: Travelers Rest, SC, 2015, pages 243–244).

poem 12. "interrupted" first appeared in *Underwater: When Encephalitis, Brain Injury, and Epilepsy Change Everything*, Chris Maxwell (Travelers Rest, SC: True Potential, 2017, 123-5).

poem 45. "lecto Divino" first appeared in *The Penwood Review* Spring 2019, vol. 23, no.1. Used with permission.

True Potential, Inc.
PO Box 904, Travelers Rest, SC 29690
www.truepotentialmedia.com

ISBN: 9781948794909 (print)
ISBN: 9781948794916 (ebook)
LCCN:
Printed in the United States of America.

acknowledgments

thanks to family and friends—your love has helped me embrace and endure the many moments of life.

thanks to people who accept me and influence me—you have helped mentor me and guide me and forgive me through this journey.

thanks to readers and writers—you are fellow travelers in this world of words.

thanks to my editors, my publisher, and my marketing teams—paul and jim and dianne and steve and many others, i can never thank you enough.

thanks to my Creator, my Listener, my Peace—You have guided me and held me and dared me in this painfully healing adventure we call life. thank You.

Contents

introduction: embracing now

this now, only here for a moment,
is brief.
i hope to notice it.
this now is like a tiny poem,
the pace, the chances,
the moods, the mystery,
the turns, the endings.
though brief,
each now can, if we choose to notice,
remind us more about ourselves:
pain we feel,
hurts being held,
more pain we hide,
more hurt needing healing.
for me, writing poetry
is prayerful therapy
for more than survival.
it opens my eyes and ears
to see and hear
this now, which, though brief,
is bringing me an opportunity
to love again, to live again,
and to breathe, slowly,
with curiosity and nerve and hesitation,
cherishing the wonder nearby.
i ask you to join me.
together, in this poetic stride called life,
let us embrace the now,
this very brief, very real,
very brilliant now.

1. a blessing

i remember hearing the blessings prayed
before every meal every day
of my life.
whatever the location, menu, environment,
whoever the fellow eaters,
whenever the time:
mouths opened,
voices requested blessings from God before
mouths opened
to taste the food
we desired,
as the smell lured our hunger toward tasting.

we waited. prayer first. that was that.
a ritual. a responsibility. a thing.

these days, we still pray prayers
of blessings before beginning
to eat. not everyone does.
many who did no longer do.

i don't think hell waits on those who miss
a blessing-before-meal-time prayer,
but i do cherish the tradition.

it's like a spiritual dietary reminder:
there's more here.
there's more here
than food we see and smell
and touch and taste.
there's more here
than calories and cholesterol.
there's more here
than time of day,

place at the table,
silverware and napkins,
cups and courtesy.

there's a reminder needed, often forgotten.
God is God.
we aren't. our meals aren't.
our possessions aren't.
our pleasure isn't.

a brief pause to give thanks,
requesting blessings from above or beside,
can shift focus,
can redirect attention,
can lure obsessions away
from me and us and this and now
to Him, to them, to there, to then.

praying the blessing prior
to beginning to taste
reminded me of another
blessing prayed.
i heard it often in my childhood
as ministers
concluded services with
a blessing, a benediction.

derived from God's prayer of blessing
in the narrative of
moses the leader, aaron his brother,
all the priests from aaron's side of the family,
and a nation of chosen ones
called, rejected, captured, and rescued,
a model clearly and regularly repeated,
the rhythmic flow of a national blessing
now coming here
for us to hear

how we, too, can be recipients
and receive blessings from God.
God told moses
what to tell aaron and his sons
as how to say a blessing
for an entire nation.
the words from there and then,
and from my childhood in
quiet, calm, reverent
settings, stated by clergy wearing robes,
and from here and now,
on this day of
holding devices which connect to a world,
hearing voices from around the world,
hoping nations can live as one world,
i hear the blessing here;
i read it, pray it, study it, state it aloud.

a benediction, a prayer of blessings.
the Lord bless you and keep you?

bless? that divine gift,
near or far, noisy or silent,
directly or indirectly,
bringing good days of
life and health and well-being
to individuals and communities,
to many and few,
to that nation and to us. today.
keep? to shelter His people,

to hold His people,
to be with them, with us, and to
never let them, or us, go.

make His face shine? the shining
face of God indicates His
acceptance and favor.

be gracious? instead of ungracious,
please, we pray and proclaim,
be gracious unto them and to us.

turn His face toward you?
the shifting and lifting of the Lord's face
indicates His countenance of grace,
mercy revealed in body language,
expression, tone, eyes
seeing gladly, joyfully. accepting
and blessing.

give you peace? shalom, we crave
as they craved. wellbeing, well living.

ending the benediction's ending
i plea for a reality of this blessing.

peace,
deep and internal and
external and pleasant
peace.

face,
His face, glancing here, now,
and desiring time with me,
all clear and obvious
from the expression on His
face.

keep,
them and us and all,
in need of safety and healing,
in search of love and joy and peace,
in a wild race for importance, please
keep.

may that blessing prayed
through so many centuries
in so many languages
apply to us today.
however You choose to fit it here,
please do.

bless us. keep us.
shine Your face upon us.
give us peace.
now and forever.
amen.

2. night in the morning

sleep stopped herself abruptly.
ending her duties too early,
leaving me little influence
as my tricks for relaxing and returning
didn't succeed.

enough, she felt, i guess,
along this quest
of thinking and rethinking
about past life and present life
and a future of unknown narratives
in now.
enough, for now, i assume sleep felt,
as she departed and left me listening again
to birds who also woke too early for me and
my rigid routine, for me and
my crafted clock of sleep and rest.
listening again to the fan circling and
the noisemaker attempting to assist in
my conflict of
noise needed to cover noise
as i hear so not to hear
to sleep and not to wake.
though my effort failed,
or, at least in the context of nowness,
didn't follow the script of my own making.
debbie slept, her breathing competing
in the battle of sounds so early or so late
in my attempt at sleeping
or praying or writing or
almost anything else now.

i thought of three sons
so   grown   up   now,

so   far   away   now,
that they aren't here to wake and talk
or play again like days ago and years ago.

so i write. i write
asking sleep to return, failing,
while also enjoying now,
the nothingness of this, of hearing,
of darkness so bright with the more
and the real and the known and the unknown.

i write as a means to an end or
as a life itself. calming. peaceful.

a sleep of a different kind,
in this typing letters and words and lines
in the brightness of darkness at 4:18 am.

thinking is different now.
praying is different now.
listening is different now.

but am i?

3. the door

a rectangular out.
a passage tall enough, wide enough, but closed.
if i had never seen a door
and known it to be a door,
what would these lines mean to me?
dark streaks on a white wall?
why the small shine of gold, an orb
halfway down (up?) inside the right shady line?

i know, because i have known doors.
i have found them open and walked through them,
found them locked and knocked upon them.
i have slammed them.
i know this meaning of escape from the present place.
i can stand, walk toward.
i can grab the gold globe and turn.
i can pull the rectangle.

at the moment a new world appears. voices, muffled
behind the closed door, sound clear. sights, hidden
by the closed door, reflect light that leaps
to my eye-socket camera that sends
data to my brain that translates
the light into understandable images.

this world and that. inside and out.
a cut of wood separating one room for another
a decision and an action: behold!
the worlds spanned by simple work.
doorways block and bridge. they keep us out and allow us in;
exclude and include. in this they are subordinate;
the purpose they serve depends on us.
we close. they say, "no."
we open. they say, "yes."

remember them
in your personal history.
front, back, bedroom, bathroom doorways.
in the childhood house, in the first house
as a spouse.
when you walked through holding an infant
grown from your seed.

read about them in scripture—doorways
as illustrations, as experiences.
door of the heart:
Jesus outside knocking, seeking access.
doors of the lips:
God as guard.
a door of faith,
a door of learning,
a door of opportunity.

the hebrew slaves put blood atop doors to save their skins.
the psalmist penned his preferences to keep
the door of God's residents.
the Savior claimed to be the door,
the only door, to
the real world.

are they alive? what secrets
do they, can they, hold?
which will we open?
which will we shut, slam, ignore?
which are spirit?
which are flesh?

some lead in; some lead out. our
choice. what we are doing and where we are going.
today, i need
blood to paint the top,
patience to stand watch at God's house. i need

faith-ears to hear the faint knocking at the heart-door,
a Sentry to guard my mouth-door,
courage to leap through the door to the real world.

today, i need to stand, walk toward,
escape this present place. dark streets and white walls,
gold shining: me
grabbing, turning, pulling.
in one act an exit and an entry.
i pray this is the right rectangle. it's
tall enough, wide enough.
but will it open?
indeed, it will.
for it is
the door
of God's designing.

4. in the middle of your hurry

in the middle of your hurry,
things didn't go just right.
an unexpected disaster interrupted
your agenda.
an unpredicted surprise blocked the streets
of your scheduled adventure.
an illness, the weather,
an accident, the economy, a sick child,
an unpleasant call, a rude response, a flat tire, a painful memory,
a day when things just didn't go right.

today, set an appointment with a place of rest.

take a nap.

pause a moment to remember—not complete a task,
clean a room,
fix a problem,
or change the world in thirty seconds.

pause. just a moment.

to remember.

to remember what matters most.

to remember yourself and your God.

to remember your children need you healthy,
not as a driven perfectionist.

to remember that a little bit of rest can give you
many more days of wonder.

5. fans: if only for a moment

characters appear resembling a crafted gage,
ready to perform in their place on stage,
harsh in sequence, then a gentle grin,
finding ways to connect within.
those faces staring as the cravings are clear,
an audience desires performance here:
their hunt for a way to say
goodbye to a day like today,
if only for a moment.

athletes sweat in the summer heat,
seeking to reach an impressive feat:
a home run here, a strikeout there,
all to accomplish the greater dare,
as fans pay much to cheer their team,
forgetting the day in a ball game dream,
their hunt for a way to say
goodbye to a day like today,
if only for a moment.

the concert starts just a little late
but the crowd is fine for this stunning date.
the music clicks, then the cheers begin,
an audience hoping this will never end.
the entertainment drug feeling like a cure,
denying reality to follow the lure:
their hunt for a way to say
goodbye to a day like today,
if only for a moment.

6. a brief poem

l
 e
  s
   s
c
 a
  n
b
 e
m
 o
  r
   e.

in a world of many words and endless presentations
we might serve better by shortening
a song, a story, a sermon, a show.
the true and deep meaning
can surprise and mean even
more by
ending unexpectedly.
now.

7. the minor prophets

i struggle to pronounce or spell their names.
under the category of
minor prophets,
in comparison, of course, to the
major prophets,
they include stories of conflict,
as all good stories do,
and hope,
as all good stories should.

i struggle to understand or fully grasp all
they said. and did.
minor prophets,
merging painful truth with unfailing love,
offering instructions and corrections,
and we have the honor
of reading their stories.
listening in.
learning from.

i wish i could meet them,
or at least see their pictures.
i want to know their facial expressions,
body language, tone of voice.
but we can imagine.
amid the skirmishes, we can imagine.

hosea—a name to remind
the people of salvation.
joel—a name to remind
them of Yahweh who is God, their Lord.
amos—a name to remind
them of the need
to carry, to be born, to be carried by God for life.

obadiah—a name to remind
them of a servant of God, a servant of the Lord.
jonah—a name to remind
them of peace, like that of a dove.
micah—a name to remind
them of a question: who is like God?
nahum—a name to remind
them of comfort or the Comforter.
habakkuk—a name to remind
them of an embrace.
zephaniah—a name to remind
them of that which is
hidden by God.
haggai—a name to change the mood and remind
them to be festive.
zechariah—a name to remind
them of being remembered by God.
malachi—a name to remind
them that he is "My messenger."

salvation is needed and available
through Yahweh.
it is more than rescue and release;
it is being born and carried by God.
it is being a servant,
living the life of a servant of the Lord
and His people.
it is flowing like a dove to bring peace
to those needing peace.
who is like this God?
no one else.
Him and Him alone. and,
He includes those
He has chosen
to speak for Him to His people.
He comforts.
He embraces.

He hides.
He celebrates.
He remembers.
He speaks,
sending His word
through His selected voices
to His chosen people.

to hear Him.
to obey Him.
to receive His comfort and embrace.
to remember He has remembered.

those twelve. faces, voices, hearts, minds, stories.
minor prophets under major assignments.

oh, hosea, i am in need of salvation.
oh, joel, can i spend a moment, just a moment
with the Lord?
will He accept me?

oh, amos,
i cannot carry this life and this me alone;
will He carry me?

oh, obadiah, serving is the calling;
will i hear it?
will I respond?

oh, jonah, can we think today of a peaceful dove
instead of a large fish?

oh, micah, no one, really,
no one is like our God.

oh, nahum, today we need the Comforter
to calm us.

oh, habakkuk, today we crave
to be embraced.

oh, zephaniah, though distant and hidden,
God is God.

oh, haggai, amid the reverence and repentance
today we need a celebration.

oh, zechariah, dear God, will you remember me
but not my many faults?

oh, malachi, am i also called by You?
am i also invited to state Your message?

those twelve names and their meanings.
to me, now.
to us, here.

detached and unique and intriguing.

teaching them. teaching us.

i struggle to pronounce or spell their names.
i struggle to understand or fully grasp all they said.
but i know i need them.
the minor prophets:
their words,
their warnings,
their names.

8. a song

mama stole my bible.

seriously. i know it was mine—it had my name on it.

but what could i do?
mama's smile had a song in it.
a song of joy and kindness and humility. her smile was
singing a song to me about
how many bibles i already had at a young age and
how that one was really perfect for her.

now, many years later, my sisters and i look at
all the notes mama wrote on my bible.
i mean, her bible.

so, how does that story relate to a book chapter titled, "a song"?
mama related to it.

to me, so much of mama's life was like music.
songs of hope and healing in the middle of
her battles with cancer. the music she heard and the rhythm of
her conversations and the melodies of
her prayers.

and our family loved the beauty of
songs and stories.
funny stories and serious stories.
sad songs and love songs.
we realized they demonstrated life.

some of mama's humorous,
unexpected, unpredicted songs are
similar to what we all do as kids.
unfortunately, we often "outgrow it."

i'm not asking that we all live childish, immature lives.
but maybe things would be a little better if we kept
the eager joy, the wonder, and the songs
of our childhood as our play lists of life.

9. time flies when you're having sons

by taking a little time to reflect and pause,
we might not rush past the now.
by appreciating the messy yards as we gently guide our kids toward
better habits,
we might find wonder and grace in times of correction and teaching.
by looking back at
their younger days and our younger days
with grace serving as a lens to see through,
we might be surprised.

surprised by the wonder of eyes glaring back,
memories embedded in our minds,
and songs sung in the kitchen.
surprised by how quickly was a decade's visit in our house.
surprised by how deep the pain, how pleasant the joy, how weak we
all are.

but in this world of surprises,
let us enjoy now.
let's not miss the now, this now, right now.
it is only here for a moment.

seeing the counselors,
praying in the morning,
noticing the beauty around here,
balancing structure with surprises,
visiting our past houses and offices,
listening to a bird singing,
watching the rabbit early in the morning,
seeing the deer hurry their way by,
standing in that very long line before boarding a very long flight,
feeling the tension of paying bills,
worrying about what type of world our kids have entered:
be still.

beside calm waters,
be still.
no, it isn't easy.

yes, time flies where you're having sons.
and daughters.
when you're having fun.
and pain.

but as it flies at such a remarkable speed,
slow yourself where you are.
and love the wonder.
this wonder.
now.

this is the only time you'll visit this moment.

don't miss it.

10. the dying

the week ended.
the week merging celebration and accusation ended.

weeks do that.
they begin their sprint then rush toward a conclusion.
like stories, our weeks contain components of
drama and tension and conflict and romance and resolution.
to pause during our weeks helps:
we notice the fragments,
we see the invisible,
we imagine the wonder,
we gaze beyond the obvious.
we believe.
while doubting and questioning,
we choose to believe.
when feeling nothing much at all,
we believe.

even when we watch a Hero punished.

even when we turn our back on our Hero.

even when we hide, barely able to notice our Hero dying.

even when the conflict and tension appear to indicate our selected
Hero became the victim.

Christ's followers found themselves not sitting
on our comfortable seats
in the theater many years later. they weren't standing to sing
a reverent song in remembrance of a distant holiday.
they were there as it occurred.
their screen was real time.
their ears heard;

their eyes saw;
their emotions felt.
their lives—risking all to pause and follow
by chasing the dreams of a single figure in this drama—appeared
to be ending also.

but we must pause here.
we must not rush past this part of the story.
if we revisit this scene often enough,
if we taste the reminders of Holy Communion deeply enough,
if we image the bloody depiction realistic enough,
we let sacraments bring faith and hope and love.
we allow death to fetch us life.

how? because from the scene of Christ's cruel death comes
a segment of this narrative that gives us
deeper reason to pause,
that offers us a
larger purpose for mentally noticing
all the wonder these pages have offered
as realities in the present.

11. today or tomorrow or yesterday

staring north,
obsessed with possibilities,
i glance, craving a view through
clouds of interruptions and uncontrollables,
but notice little.

worries about tomorrows
limit accomplishments in todays,
but i still stare, glaring
out the window toward the future.
or, at times, turn my head to
see through windows in other rooms
reminding me of my perceptions
of historical realities. but
i see only now. slight images
which might indicate
completed pages or future possibilities
should not rob me of this moment
that is with me and beside me.
though tomorrow isn't here
i bring it
as here as possible
to plan, to prepare,
which is all good
if it is
not controlling me or stealing away
my now.

tomorrow isn't here.

i shouldn't force it here.

it will come.

i should expect and be ready
while dedicated to each segment
in now's story.
if not
my eyes will stare at the distant images,
those tomorrows of maybes
or these yesterdays of whys,
so cloudy, so covered,
and inhibit my view of this
moment's beauty.

i'm unsure of the impulse
when my mind illuminates
scenes from distant time:
ignorance of a scheme,
taking a dream and resurrecting it
with shouts and smiles and long walks
of many dusty miles;
can i absorb now?
can i converge thisness and thenness
in the wavering of my views
of the window and out the window?

i shall try,
with effort and intentionally.

i shall try
to avoid obsession about
yesterday or tomorrow.

i shall try
to truly be
here today.

12. interrupted

i despise being interrupted.
when speaking my portion of a conversation;
an interruption, though well-intended,
becomes a thief breaking in
and robbing my mind.

when interrupted, i feel lost at sea.
my location isn't easy to find.
where was that? where am i?
how do i locate myself again,
and my word again,
and my thoughts again?
an interruption becomes
the conclusion. my verbal adventure
stops suddenly. a wall appears.
another step feels impossible.
i wait and wait and wait
for an opening, for a memory, for a word.
nothing emerges.

finally, i locate another word
as a substitute.
or i ask for help. either way,
i do not like this. but
i'm learning this.
i am learning
this life—this life
of failure, of frustrations,
of dependence, of forgetting.
this life of interruptions.
this life with baggage.
this life at sea.
i'm adjusting to this life
of always knowing a seizure is possible.

this life with epilepsy.
it feels like a caution light
blinking and blinking.
do i stop or slow? do i turn?
i choose, usually, to
not frown when facing those facts.
i smile. people with epilepsy have boundaries,
but don't all people?
yes, we need sleep
and the care of others
and sunglasses, but
all people do. we need the caution light's reminder
of these words: be careful.
all people do.
we are unique, yet
not controlled by our conditions.

well, let's get back to the interruptions.
words, often difficult to locate in this brain,
frequently take time to be stated.
much time.
i try.
they hide.
i try hard.
they refuse to reveal themselves.
a noun. a name of a person i know.
a verb. an action i've known well and long.
hidden, distant, afar: words.
i merge memories
and mingle experiences. i try.
i fail to find words.

but the process is
worse when interrupted.
let me try and fail,
then ask for a name.
don't invade my endeavor to recall.

though, if i
sat in your seat
and listened to my weak
attempt to remember, if i
stared at a frustrated face
like my own and
craved to offer assistance,
i would interrupt. i'd bid a solution
if the situation was opposite.
i get it. but i'm helped best
when those close to me realize
they'll never fully get it.
they just choose to endure
the wait—hearing my conversation stop,
seeing my facial expressions of frustration,
desiring to rescue me from the war of forgetfulness,
hurting with me—while hidden words merge
their appearance slowly
if at all.

give me a little time even if i request otherwise.
give me a little time even when my search engine malfunctions.
give me a little time until i can invest no more effort in the adventure
of recall.
give me time underwater. and, please,
give me your acceptance even when
my attempts to remember
or stay calm or seem normal
all fail.

13. listen

listen.
to the songs,
    the birds,
      the vehicles,
        the music,
          the conversations,
            the machines,

listen.
to the food ordered at meal time,
    the umpire calling balls and strikes,
      the fans cheering,
        the planes flying,
listen.
to the piano, the guitar, the harmonica, the drums, the voices,
listen.
to the silent thoughts, the simple prayers, the kind words, the gentle smile,
listen.
listen to the good today. not just the bad.
do not only hear hate and division and bitterness and greed and pain.
hear forgiveness.
hear acceptance.
hear kind disagreement instead of hateful separation.
listen. to a need. act to meet it.
  listen. to a prayer. agree with it.
    listen. to a dream inside you. pursue it.
      listen. to luggage from your past. release it.
listen. today.
to Him and them.
  to you and me.
    to nearby and far away.
listen. today.

14. ladies in a room

i walked slowly into the room
smelling the aroma reminding me
of the assisted living environment,
lives locked inside,
uncontrollable bodies and minds,
where body function and mental reflection
fit the narrative of expecting
and being surprised, of cleaning
and becoming needy again.

i stared;
it took me a few moments to recognize
the dear lady i had known
for all my life's decades.
through shades of aging
her appearance drastically changed, but
i could tell she was her.

so well so long before.
she had changed. i had changed.

gazing, walking slowly, smelling
while breathing memories,
i talked to her directly,
while other ladies ignored or interrupted
while sitting, while staring,
and she looked at me
and smiled.

conversations reflected on history.
biographies of family members.
specific details of events:
times, places, moods.

then a sudden shift
from knowing me and our narratives
to again being the her she now is.
staring, stuttering, making
little sense, at least to my mind.

i hugged her, hearing her
laughter again.

i departed, slowly.
she stared at me, then slowly
shifted her view toward and through
the window.
this is her life
now, slowly.

15. 5:40

24 hours in a day.
1,440 minutes.
yet, with so many options available of
hours and minutes
we habitually select slots
holding two zeros at the end.
5:00 or 6:00 or 7:00 or 9:00, or if we're
risky and rebellious,
willing to settle for one zero,
we gamble for the middle
choice and elect 5:30 or 9:30.

hours and minutes abandoned,
crowds packing places and
scheduling predictable numbers,
as we avoid other numbers, rejecting
options available in addictive trends;
do we have no feelings for the
many minutes and hours ignored?

often i select the neglected slots,
maybe more for my memory
than kindness to them, or
maybe not –
none of us are totally sure of ourselves
are we?
i'm not,
but I prefer 5:40 rather than 5:00 or 6:00.
i recall the time to meet,
remembering it as if
time matters, as it
does, and should,
for me.

16. an anniversary poem

years ago you voiced
your "yes,"
you declared "i do"
as you entered new land,
a territory you'd noticed
but not known, observed
but not experienced.
but now you have,
and you continue having
opportunities of grace,
of joy,
of questions,
during this adventure
of adjusting
and embracing
life together.

your smiles and prayers,
your songs and dares,
your here and there
while shifting in times
for rhymes of now
as this anniversary arrives
and smiles back.

notice. notice this and now.
notice faces of your children.
notice dreams of your heart.
notice scars and limps and
love through each step taken,
that love so real and deep,
that love so eternal.
notice it again.
and again.

remember. rejoice.
rewind and glance again
toward, now, a
future of more meals
and music and smiles
and hugs and hands
held by one another
and the Creator
of those hands
and those hearts
which still beat
to the rhythm of
love deep and true,
for the two of you
for now and forever
in these waves
of grace.

your "yes" you
voiced years ago
is repeated again.
and again.
as years pass,
grace stays,
love stays,
here, now,
there, then,
as life together forever.

17. reverse process

final score revealed before a game begins.
verdict today, trial tomorrow.
decisions made in advance
without a chance of change
for a mind, or the minds of many:
the process is backwards.

18. old days

i remember some of them.
i miss some of them.
i know though,
i know things and people
and days change,
and ways of life
take turns toward
newness and neverness,
as memories feel like fiction
rather than real
old days.

19. results

words arrive. scenes appear.
memories surge. stories emerge,
mingling fact and fiction,
revealing altered views of
history right beside reality. but
those images appear real, feel real.
they leave marks. scars clearly
prove whatever it is they're providing.

20. hilton head

morning by the beach.
as i process, while walking on
the sand of now,
those four words cause
me to think of another one.
one word sounding similar to another word
revealing that i am actually
mourning at the beach. because of
the years, the wounds, the losses,
the scars,
this mourning on this morning
alerts my mind
as i watch the sun's shine reveal herself. sounds of birds and waves
raise answers and questions
again and again. a light
bringing brightness to the beautiful blue sky, white and gray clouds,
moon, and
a wide world. her beauty
reminds me of
the greatness around and
the weakness within.
i am small.
God is big.
the Creator crafted the art of grace.
now the shine on a face
reminds me again what i need to remember.
the world is larger than my limited vision.
my problems are small.
though they feel majestic,
they are midgets compared to
His majesty.
a morning of mourning
as prayer, as therapy, as healing.
the sun rose. i stare, small.
i surrender. all.

afternoon by the beach.
evening by the beach.
more and more and more.
the shore seems sure.
i learn. again. today.

21. five loaves and two fish

tiny ingredients for a large audience.
not enough, those two words which
often describe so many stories
of our lives.
not enough.
we seek. we hope. we pray.
we reach.
we fall.
we have
not enough.

the crowd came to hear Jesus.
the crowd came hungry,
maybe for words
but certainly for a meal.

the followers of Christ
didn't bring sufficient provision.
they wouldn't have enough to supply
their target audience
even if they'd worked in advance.
so why try?
why not ask them to bring
their gifts to
the Leader?

Jesus didn't work that way.
Jesus wouldn't fit today.

size of gift? tiny.
any return expected? none.
a child willing to assist,
however possible
with all he had.

not enough. not enough. never enough.
so seems the mental perspective
often leading our views
when hearing our news,
in our routine.

five thousand people.
two fish.
five loaves of bread.
do the math.
imagine the scene.
assume the assumptions.

but Jesus didn't do the norm.
Jesus didn't fit the mathematical model.
from little came much.
more than enough,
a reality.

and us?
can we learn about
needing, offering all, seeing a miracle?
can we learn about
giving and believing?

22. years gone

rebounding their jump shots.
pitching and catching and hitting baseballs.
passing and catching footballs.
reading books and singing songs.
listening to words spoken while hearing
ping pong percussion.
sitting together at the table.
to eat. to ask. to listen. to care.
reading the same books and talking about
what's being learned and loved and lived.

years visited, but only briefly.
experiences occurred, but quickly ended.

i cherish my now while missing my thens.

i think back.

23. always in shadows

i left the logo behind.
not needing noticeable images
to alert reminders of reality,
from colors selected and designs crafted,
in the order of achievement,
so i didn't bring it along.

i brought myself though. no logo
or image,
just me
and all traveling with me.

years of knocking on the wood,
fears of living as i should.
these weather forecasts and guesses
are not really here.

24. observing

will i glance wider
while clearly seeing now?
will i voice feelings when necessary,
and into the right ears,
while adjusting to a frantic 911 call
or a slow marathon
of treatments and more treatments,
while preferring my planned routine though
surprises bring moisture of perspiration
or tears?
will i?

will i
observe by gazing mentally,
mustering momentum toward
a better awareness of now-ness,
as a refusal to miss this one visit
of the present.

interpreting emotions
as what they are rather than
as what they aren't,
diving in when aware of water
in some ways but not all ways,
studying to know more and better,
rewiring mental ability,
the workouts of life involving
more than
physical strength
for appearance or stamina,
working the brain, the soul, the self
in an adventure of
taking a wider glance
while observing life.

and death.
the faces have names.
the numbers have stories.
the statistics are
real people, real lives, real narratives
if noticed or not.
who cares? who cares
enough to be and to do?
to observe and respond,
earnestly investing energy in
more than
jobs and stocks and assumptions
but long walks and long conversations
on days like today—
with the storms followed by a clear sky—
and in stories like ours—
with the doctor finally telling us
the news?

25. days together

prayers, songs, conversations,
ideas, questions, instructions,
inspirations, meals, confessions,
hopes, dreams, plans.
laughter and tears.
celebration and contemplation.
together today.
in place and time and
hearts, together.

what can and will
we learn?
we know of many machines,
though other devices
we fail to find
in our manufactured masterpiece
of power and more power.
times of previous attempts
to improve
we crafted crafts to assist,
but now our energy is invested
in running the mechanics we hoped would
help keep us running.

now, we're tired,
but beginning to notice
there is more.
stories are teaching us
to return
not to our songs or styles,
but return to our true reason
for being and for doing,
for who and what,
for why and how,
an empowering with purpose—to be witnesses

locally and globally,
to make, craft, design, direct,
and mentor disciples.

we are aging but young again.
we are trained but
learning anew.
we are ancient but returning to our first love.
returning, we are, together.

was that a machine moved aside?
did a face of grace take its place?
are various ages and colors
together in this now,
this new now,
this ancient and modern now,
this no-longer-addicted-to-ourselves now,
this not-trapped-inside-these-walls now,
this now of merging minds
and mingling hearts,
this now of authenticity,
this now of noise and silence?

led by the Leader rather
than our machine.
loving one another rather
than dividing.

these meetings on these days
of recalling new ways
of telling the Truth to them—
all of them, every them,
as prayers and plans place
hearts together in the time
of now
for them, for then,
for Him.

26. a healing process

denial and avoidance
are not the follow up.
facing is.
gracing is.

responding directly, wisely, calmly.
with wide vision,
long-term thinking,
and in a fitting time and
place, respond.

we respond after
recognizing reality.
rather than living in denial,
this allows a step to be taken
toward healing.
looking at what is,
what really is,
offers a realization
of the present conditions
crowding life.
our problems can be deeper
than surface revelations;
cause and effect get missed
in the habitual hurry
of our allowed escapisms.
recognize. face facts.
before anything, begin in
the moments of noticing.
and responding.

release is the next
and needed response.
not with high volume anger,

not in attack-back mode,
not seeking control,
but releasing as in
refusing to hold on to,
or be held and controlled by
those words,
those old words,
that experience,
that painful experience,
their facial expression or
tone of voice or
final punch of words.

recognize how deeply
the hurt was planted.

respond by choosing to
take action.

but let that reaction
of letting go
be an action of healing.

refuse now,
to be any longer
controlled by pains from
the past. say goodbye.

then receive;
you have room now.
your hands and heart and mind
are no longer using all
emotional muscle by
carrying the weight
of then and there,
of them and that,
but now, a new day,

a new way of thinking,
is a welcoming
with hands opened, not closed,
with possibilities and potential,
with a smile,
with eyes open, looking forward,
with heaviness thrown away,
with a new look now.
receiving love.
receiving peace.
receiving rest,
in this time, this time.

and then what? rejoice.
rejoice as recognition, response,
release, and receive guided
from defeat to freedom.
a celebration is appropriate,
a joy, unspeakable,
is this new climate,
an environment craved for
many days.
stand to sing.
sit to stare toward tomorrows
no longer trapped by yesterdays.

27. thinking before sleeping

bed, this place i cherish,
holds me as i process
the ending day
and as i preview tomorrow.
i'm unsure of too many things,
at least too many for my preference,
but i must not allow uncertainty
rob me of rest.
in this bed, on this night,
i sense a sight not
as blurry as normal.
a prayerful release.
a meditative reflection.
a view through hope.
surrender, trust, believe.
notice, observe, breathe.
swallow slowly,
inhale slowly,
exhale slowly,
eyes closed, seeing
the larger view of new
things, a determination
not forced, guided
into a trust
and sleep.

28. a letter to the rain

dear rain, i am sorry. remembering days of smiling with you, running as you soaked me, enjoying your sound. but i changed. long ago, i changed. i no longer enjoy you. this morning, while dreading a long drive during your dropping-down-upon-me agenda, i realized i've changed. i do not like you. my thoughts about you dwell on the negative experiences. when you brought hurt, when results were unpleasant, when houses were damaged, when lives ended. because of those memories, i've deleted the days we smiled together. today, i want to bring back a balanced view of you. like life, like all of it, like jobs and relationships and seasons, each companion offers pleasure and pain. laughter and tears arrive with love. birth and death both exist. as do you. you come quickly, dripping when predicted or unexpected. can i love you again? the nourishments you offer, the necessities you provide, the shifts you send: can i nod and grin rather than wishing you would go away? can i, with you and with people and with life, refuse to let storms turn me away from precipitation needed? what must i do? decide? just decide? realize my feelings but not let them control my thoughts for too long? oh, rain, drop here. fall here today. and after so many seasons, see me waiting for you and smiling.

29. hope to hear

listening to the prayer and the songs,
listening to the rain and the rap,
listening to scripture read and
listening to my imagination guess
about Jesus and His time and
His audience in the story.
did they listen?
are we listening?

my mind listens, imagining the mood
of Jesus as He hurt for the people.
rapping reality, the heart of Jesus,
He saw the crowds,
He had compassion
on them, because they were
harassed and helpless,
like sheep without a shepherd.

counseling appointments
reminded me of listening,
of the harassed and helpless,
of sheep
with or without
a shepherd.

four deaths reminded me of listening.
franz mascarenhas, eugene peterson,
charlie thomas, chad floyd:
four very different narratives
all fitting the larger story,
the larger questions and answers.

as we changed clocks to add an hour,
i pondered again the thought

dr scott ellington said last week:
"you will never grow up until you decide to."
i hear and process
the confrontation elijah cortez

wrote and rapped to us:
"whatcha doin with your soul,
He paid way too high a price,
for all of us to go
and throw
away our life."

mad, sad, glad: i felt
and feel
each emotion.
madness and sadness,
those relatives
which hold hurt deeply inside.
gladness, often absent, is here
amid the rain of sadness,
like a sun covered in clouds.
harassed and helpless, sad to glad,
what do we need to do,
who do we need to become?
seeking answers, really, for this question:
what it means to be a follower of Christ?
and these questions:
how does Jesus forgive our poor decisions?
how do we change our lifestyles?
Jesus is, answering those thoughts
as the Answer Himself, inviting
us all to the adventure.
that's the decision to grow up,
to receive the invitation,
to follow the Guide,
to be developed by the Mentor,
to be loved by the Lover.

trying to listen now
to Jesus and His time and become
His audience,
to live within His story.

listening . . . are we?
listening . . . are we?

30. in the back

an impulse can become destructive.
or it can deliberately begin
an extravagant pummeling of madness,
a process of healing which
can help vanish a stagnated landscape
of life, letting flares
of liturgy draw astonishing resilience.
different results. different moods.
slopes, similar initial
tendencies, trends, feelings.
outcome? segments.
often in segments.
voices unnerve bewildered prodigals
like me, vulnerable,
glancing toward grace
in the similar,
perceiving richness though stumbling
in the ordinary,
recognizing, refreshed.
details hidden, perceived,
as another survivor is given new sight,
disguised as a stranger,
darkening no more,
dread gone,
savoring simplicity,
i shall cling now, and trust,
though decayed, found,
i shall flow, composing
sparse shadows,
not exempt,
convergence, glimmering,
contrasting obvious,
ancient and desperate,
deems unnoticed, merging and

confronting capacity,
hearing ancient sounds
ringing instantly
in a moment of acquisitions.

31.of the night

there's a light in the crack of the curtain,
resembling an eye glancing
through the dark,
reminding me of a tiny moon
shaped as a circle.
not sure of the glare
but i stare,
knowing it is there
for my final view of the night,
my final view of the night.

there's a noise in the air from the bypass,
resembling percussion louder
than preferred,
reminding me the drivers travel
deep into the dark.
not sure of the source,
but i hear
knowing it is there
for my final sounds of the night,
my final sounds of the night.

there's a thought in the measure of my mind,
resembling a song continuing
its rhythm,
reminding me of my dialogue
with the Divine.
not sure of how answers
specifically arrive,
but believing He is listening
to my final prayers of the night,
my final prayers of the night.

32. 499 miles

time travels while we're apart,
this cadence of
miles between our faces,
that separation through locations.
we have obligations with
so many
other people and other jobs,
so many
other lives and other things,
so many
other lists and other tasks,
and yet,
conversations converge
like a continual dialogue
never divided by the
decades of distance.
we begin again
as if we stayed
at the same table,
aging, changing, developing,
gracefully and peacefully,
as the same people
still near each other,
to laugh,
to ask questions,
to pray,
to eat,
to offer opinions,
to say
words which will be forgotten,
but remembered, really,
in deeper ways
as days
visit and depart,

as we
visit and depart,
as if
499 miles creates
no conclusion at all,
just fresh chapters
of more words
for more stories
on more times
together, wherever
we are told we are today.

33. morning prayers

i request though knowing
Your final method of delivery
and timing
provide a better plot
than my assumed
and initially preferred result.

chemistry between us,
between me and You
and the many more in our family,
occurs more frequently
when trust enters the room.

so this morning,
i petition large requests,
holding nothing back.
knowing transparency is allowed,
i voice various pleas
as sincere prayers
and deep desires,
while knowing Your answers
will arrive at a different time,
in a different way,
as a different result,
than my limited vision can see.

is that faith?
requesting, releasing, trusting?
giving thanks before
the story ends?
rejoicing amid the tension
of the moment?

is that faith?

if so, help me believe, please.
and help my unbelief.
for my morning prayer,
i ask You
all of this
knowing i know little,
but knowing that knowing You
and Your love
and Your wisdom
is really enough.
amen.

34. uneven surfaces

the sign predicted the status
waiting for us.
straight lines and simple turns
aren't ahead. the ground
isn't even.
like life, the surface,
our place of dependence,
isn't even.
meaning what?
a serious concern
or a disruption of our preferences?
actually, expectations can
go unmet.
often, security doesn't
seem secure.
i don't expect casualties,
just adjustments,
leaning slightly when needed,
with curves and angles
staring, not moving
as they force our moves
along the surface.

35. above ground

sitting together above ground,
calmed by the lake's sounds,
asking one another questions,
listening intensely, intentionally,
we've moved from surface dialogue
on the ground of casual conversations
holding little real value
to now:
narratives we held inside for far too long,
stories we need, though resist, to tell.
we breathe deeply and hesitate before
being capable of initiating
a courageous entrance
into the remarks we prefer to deny
but need to confess.

we walked up steps to sit in the chairs
of an elderly tree stand to stare
and engage in the issues
of life, of lives,
of our lives.

the tree looks, feels, like a giant.
ancient but here.

our topics sound, feel, like giants.
painfully healing.

uncertainty sits with us.
hope gazes into the lake,
as our eyes see boats below
and planes above,
as our ears listen
intentionally to the intensity

of lives
clouded with uncertainty.
i believe in you.
your gifts, your talent, your will.
your dreams, your hopes, your art:
how you wash the feet of others
by being there,
by listening, by guiding.

but do you? do you believe
in the called you, the gifted you,
the empowered you?

doubts dwell nearby
in the breeze of self-talk,
in your mind bombarded by
pains from the past,
questions amid the present,
uncertainty about the future.

sitting by you,
hearing what's stated and what isn't,
i believe. in you. in your importance.
in your now. in your next pages.

as we often do, we prayed.
eyes open to creation's beauty,
we prayed, hoping to believe.
i do. i believe in you.

will you join me
with that view of you?

above the service,
staring forward,
choosing hope,
as the wind of grace

blows away the unneeded
thoughts, questions, and numbness.
please see you,
and believe you
are important.
your future includes fears
being released through tears
and a new adrenaline,
real and genuine,
driven with considered motives
rather than shallow waves,
giving you
the new view
you crave.
your calling. your importance.
your being. not always your doing.
see that way.
stay that way.
and believe.

above ground.
listening. and deeply,
smiling, now.

36. a poem for christmas

thanksgiving and christmas,
new year's eve and new year's day,
all arriving in this sudden segment
of life,
on days concluding school terms
or days beginning fresh times
as the calendars and clocks
carried in our hands
carry us, drag us,
as we breathe, barely,
frantically finding autumn
in passing, then winter,
in seasonal show of sudden shifts
amid our normalcy.
what can we do?
now, what can we do?
can we rest while time rushes by?
can we cherish more than
food on plates and
lights on trees and
colors all around?
can we choose to glance back,
recalling a purpose for gatherings
during the rush?

turning minds backwards,
hearing tales told and stories read,
imagining sights and sounds,
within narratives of a mary
and a joseph, a baby,
angels and shepherds,
animals and mystery.
glancing again and again,
as we think back,

at the child.
a birth promised but impossible.
a birth with little room
but celebrated.
a birth in a setting of
weakness and poverty and
silence and noise and
no room and this room and
impossible and real and
remembered now.
now. here. in our hurry,
memories glancing back,
songs raising volume
in various languages and voices,
celebrating a belief seeming
impossible, a reality feeling
nearby, a baby believed
to give them all,
to give us all,
life.

37. two voices

i expected rejection.
my expectations were correct.
my effort did not receive applause;
it did not receive a smile;
it did not receive approval.
why should it? i cannot succeed,
achieve, complete:
that's the collection of words from
that voice replaying regularly
in my mind.
he walked away. i stayed, wishing
i could make him happy.

but, after moments passed,
i glanced around the room
and saw a Stranger nearby.
He looked up, making eye contact
with a calm but serious facial expression.
He looked familiar, like a former best friend
or a distant relative i deeply missed.
He stood and walked toward me.
He told me Who He was.
i felt afraid and bowed my head.
with His gentle arms He lifted me up and
with His kind words He declared
a very different evaluation than
the voice i'd precisely heard.
this Voice was God.
that voice was condemnation.

why do i so often settle for the
initial voice?
which one should i believe and receive?
what can i do to

become better
at realizing i am not
being demanded to
become better
before gentle arms and kind words
rewire my thinking and my living?

i sat. i stayed.
He sat beside me. He smiled,
His face appearing pleased to be
with me then, doing nothing
but just what He wanted all along.

38. inviting worship to this table

can you come to the table
and bring your ancient hymns?
i listened and learned when young,
though style and form did not thrill me.
i distanced myself from you, then
invited you back.
many of your songs' depths
reveal our beliefs. we need you.

can you come to the table
and bring your songs of praise?
i began hearing you in your beginning,
the style and form fit my own journey.
i need to memorize your truth, so
i invite you back.
in many of your songs the simplicity
repeats scripture. we need you.

can you come to the table
and bring your modern worship?
i found you as you found me,
in style and form we connected quickly.
i've distanced myself from you, slightly,
disliking extremes of performance.
but many of your songs fit the psalmist's
honesty, variety. we need you.

can you come to the table
and bring your biblical psalms?
i memorized and prayed your poetry
when young,
imagining style and form.
i need you as i pray and question,
praise and confess.

though many of your songs would not
fit in our preferred styles, we need you.

we need each of you.
i need each of you.
remind me again that worship
isn't to be my fix, my drug, my thrill.
i'm not to worship you, worship,
but to worship God
in various forms and styles.
worship through music
is to release inner pain
with reverence for the goal
of honoring God,
not me or us.
our feelings can be released here
but they aren't to control
what we do or why or how we do it.

at this table, i seek to learn from
each of you.
teach me to worship,
in spirit, in truth,
and not let this endeavor
be about me
or for me.

but Him. just Him.
at this table, can you come and
teach me to truly worship
Him?

39. 31 degrees

slightly below freezing,
the air alerts my need to grab
a skull cap to cover my bald head,
the place cold air feels most potent,
so i do so
quickly, grabbing keys for a ride
from small town to a larger town
on a friday in december,
for a meeting in the cold climate
with a friend whose warm heart
seems to always care,
deep and genuine care,
whatever coats and gloves
and covers for our heads
we use,
he sees
through them all,
warming us with his acceptance.

40. all i can do

no, i don't know exactly how you feel.
no, i can't completely comprehend.
no, i won't fully relate.

i've never
gone through your painful situation.

i have
gone through my painful situations
and continue doing so.

but every story, every scar,
is unique.
so, i'll not nod and make inappropriate
statements like, "i've been there" or
"we all know what that's like."

i haven't.
we don't.

though different, i can do this:
i can listen.
i can be here and stay,
listening to your story.
i can offer my attention.

at times i might cry,
at times i might nod,
at times i might glance away,
but i'm here.
not as a cure.
as a companion,
a fellow traveler,
on a different route

but with my own wrecks.
yes, i will listen.
yes, i will stay.
yes, i will pray.

is that okay?
though that is all i can do,
is that okay?

41. begin again

now is the time. begin.
for the first time, begin.
or, for the tenth time, begin again.
with love and humility and courage
holding hands, begin.
release frustrations.
release fear.
guided by God-given dreams, begin.
uncontrolled by past mistakes, begin.
now.
it is time.

42. segments in time

long walks and honest talks,
delicious meals and sincere smiles,
joyful songs and peaceful silence,
time, in segments, passing
amid the avalanche of perplexity.

leaves, branches, limbs: colors.
a breeze, an aroma, a sky: nature.

like a teaser, time carries us
rapidly, daring us to glare nearby,
to glance at grace
beside us, each moment,
beside us, an enigma
to notice, to know.

the context of landscape,
the eagerness of next,
the gaze of a glimpse:
seeing tiny parts
of a majestic puzzle.

am i praying?
am i learning?
am i worshiping?
am i waiting?
am i serving?
am i listening?
whatever discipline i'm practicing,
i cherish. and i breathe.

this moment, a visit,
to never return,
is a spectacle
of divinity.

43. forward progress

my speed isn't good today.
my endurance isn't available today.
my strength isn't solid today.
no sprint. no marathon. no muscle.

my effort toward the far land
would not be sustainable.
a push for distance
would not be wise.

but   a   step.   just   one.
one   tiny   step   forward,
not   back,
is   progress.
though   that   is   all,
that   is   okay,   today,
to
be
all.

44. shadows

the assembling of shadows,
reflections in black and white,
images incorrectly displaying
size and shape,
correctly and curiously
declaring the presence
of more.

light shines from a location,
stares forward,
acting like artists crafting
their own interpretation
of the world.

inverted. intriguing.

this blocking of light,
this reverse projection,
these dimensions,
these reminders
of what is here and what is not.

visibility. volume.

shadows seen, felt, known,
can serve to
illustrate faith,
positively or negatively,
as the changing of a view
of more.

45. lectio Divina

reading a passage of scripture
slowly and carefully.
very slowly.
very carefully.

praying as conversation
with God.
communicating to and with God,
within the text.
opening with words
and without words.

meditation.
deeply thinking.
staying within the passage
and refusing to pass it by.
telling the mind to wait;
not letting natural lures
move the thoughts away.
staying there.

contemplation.
resting a while
in God's presence,
in God's Word,
in God.

an action?
to go now.
to go next.
to go and do likewise.
from learning it
and resting in it
to living it out.

a time of divine reading
intended to transform
a person like me,
like you,
by receiving the
Voice of God
from the
Word of God.

lectio: reading.
meditatio: reflection.
oratio: response.
contemplatio: rest.

amid the madness
of our hurry,
can we open the
ancient and alive Word,
welcoming guidelines
to slow our pace
and receive Truth,
in a reading of the Divine?

46. curtains

cover me, hide me,
prohibit me from seeing through
or being seen.

limitations, intended.

what if a decision was made
to open them?
what would change?

the world exists
even behind the curtains.
but who knows of it?

imagination
becomes normality
when the same
stays the same,
and curtains remain.

to stand, to walk, to change:
curtains can open, can alter,
can allow eyes to see through
those things
which changed from
safety to control.

goodbye fear.

hello light.

the outside world is now
inside my own world.

47. breakfast percussion

the early morning sounds
of a spoon grabbing bites
of cereal in rhythm,
like a daily habit
on time
in place
where the taste and nourishment
aren't all there, is here.
an experience is here.
a cadence of talking
while eating breakfast
before others wake,
before the sun shows her face,
is here.
habit, yes.
ritual, yes.
but an addictive freedom
to taste, to see, to hear, to believe
my beliefs aren't false
assumptions or preferences,
but truth.
a truth
verified, more real to me
while playing habitual percussion
on time
in place
with spoon
for the early morning sounds.

48. war of worship

the war within our worship
misses many major points
as we debate on
styles and preferences
including God to make our case.
but just in case we care
about more than our desires,
wouldn't it be wonderful
to worship once again,
in Spirit and in Truth,
together and alone,
with music and in silence,
while refusing to hold tightly
to ourselves?
we've reduced the size
and meaning of this large
holy endeavor and
crafted selfish minor punches
while ignoring holiness,
community, diversity, history,
reverence, and celebration.
should emotions control decisions?
should popularity?
should appeal?
should appearance?
or are there deeper issues
to still consider
within the playlists
of our trends?

can i choose a menu
of ancient and modern,
of long and short,
of loud and soft,

of a biblical text repeated and
a personal confession
creatively crafted,
of a large choir and
a soloist?
can i choose them all,
at various times and places,
electing not only one,
but the many,
with hymns and poems
and art and prayers
and phrases of praise
as all forms of declaring truth
and releasing feelings
and moving myself out of the way
and shifting focus
to our Father, Son, Spirit.

this is not about us.

49. false start

an abrupt endeavor in pursuit of pleasure
can initiate dangerous habits,
can cling, refusing departure,
like poison with a fine initial taste.

violence, though slow, mingles
within a masked face
proposing a smile, though
fake reality shall diminish,
eventually, true reality arrives.

obscurity, step by step.
camouflaged habitually
becoming a routine.

can't this end?
can't life begin again?
transparency in the right setting,
transformation in the waiting,
conclusion of a story and
beginning of another, a better.
finish it. initiate the new now,
in humility, with help,
nerves shaking and head nodding,
brave grit with grace received.

let's not count the score
in round one.

50. how much longer?

how much longer
do i have to wait?
is this wrath,
or is it fate?
is this a result
of my own mistake?
i'll ask again
and linger more;
i'll knock at midnight
on Your door,
but the unknown
battles me again.
unsure of the what
and unknowing the when;
how much longer
do i have to wait?

51. making a point

interrupted mid-sentence,
ignoring points and emphasis and
intentions to continue a conversation,
carrying dialogue from conflict
to a win-win, then
an experience to mend
the deep wounds from dark days,
but i wasn't offered that chance.
like a trance,
your control concluded the conversation
with little else but you,
just you,
and your mood and your point made,
as always.
i wasn't allowed to complete a sentence.
that, in itself,
completed a sentence.
the same old sentence.
again.

52. more words

words.

           words written,

     read,

prayed   before   sleep.

     words

          as

               reminders,

      as revelations,

          as confessions.

    words of grief.

     words of peace.

       words of hope.

creative,

             poetic,
        kind words.

   for   now,

      before

        sleep,

           words.

53. Jesus and a platform

an agent and a publicist
watched the crowd growing
as they waited on three c.e.o.s
from key publishing companies
to arrive for that day's encounter.

Jesus, the rumors indicated,
was walking their way.

they struggled to accurately
define His platform.
the poor, those unlikely to invest
in this fascinating endeavor,
continued stepping forward,
walking their way to hear a Leader
appearing interested
in those rejected.

but rejection wasn't an option
for this agent.
the Jesus rumors triggered
momentum, and now
was time for capturing
the model of promotional power.
crowds continued coming.
editors could be seen
in the audience;
the agent grinned at the publicist.
they cherished this tension
of bids and better bids,
of comparisons and competition,
of the Voice of One
calming storms and
raising the dead and

claiming to be King.
momentum rising.
audience enlarging.
an agreement awaiting.
they felt the mood,
like magical motion.
emotions were obvious
as religious leaders
and political leaders
stared, waiting, watching,
and families brought
sick relatives,
and all tribes seemed to merge:
when have tax collectors, priests,
teachers, prostitutes, and
children all mingled beside
military might
waiting for the sight
of One claiming to be a Savior?
rarely, if ever, at least
not at this level.

the agent smiled more
as the Teacher appeared,
though the smile diminished slightly
as Christ's appearance seemed not
as luring
as expected.
but smiles returned, eyes winked,
when stories were told
and people applauded or asked
questions which were answered by
more stories while people
and more people
continued arriving.
Jesus didn't preach long.
Jesus took time to mingle

with a few who would never
purchase His books or
listen to His podcasts;
the agent and publicist
made eye contact again, and
looked toward editors,
seeking to read their minds,
while potential numbers of sales
occupied their thoughts.

it was near time,
time to meet with Jesus.

momentum was high.
numbers were huge.
potential was ideal.

they planned to interview Jesus,
hearing His heart
of future goals and agendas,
of probable crowds and miracles to come,
of new stories to lure buyers,
of platform power,
as editors and c.e.o.s took notes
to begin their offers.
money waited in their minds as
they waited for Jesus.

but He never came.
He left.
Jesus left.

the crowd and Christ's disciples
were still around.
but He wasn't.

Jesus, surprising the culture,
was walking away.

He'd walked away,
crying about the throng of hurting ones
and feeling nauseous as His eyes
made contact with
belligerent buyers and sellers.

His mind seemed to
dwell on different goals.

His purpose seemed to
not fit the day's market.

the agent shook his head.
the editors walked away.
the publicist looked frustrated.

but a lonely lady finally felt loved
for the first time in her life.

an alone Jesus
prayed to His father,
thankful for offering healing
while escaping the momentum
in the marketplace.

54. confession

power struggles,

tribalism or belonging,

rigorous dissonance:

inventory and distance,

environmental exposure,

depressive disclosure.

many reactive realities,

designing and disrupting

capabilities and availability.

transparency and honest conversations.

unmasked, unwrapped, uncovered,

unscripted, unrehearsed, unleashed.

this kind of kindness is

usually kept away from us.

unless we face truth and

view surrender as victorious.

what would you say?
what could you say?
what should you say?

unknown hidden listener
unaffected by brutality

voiced awkwardly,
in place

for a structure
for this.

the refusal to hold, to maintain.
the determination to cast away
correctly, appropriately,

now, no longer waiting for the

perfect time or place,

instead, choosing this as the

setting to become free.

55. will You hear?

will You hear their hurting cries
and know them,
understand them,
respond to them,
even when wounds are not
clearly described?

i tried but failed
to fully grasp the depth
of their lesions.

i try but struggle,
and never know
if i show them the love
i should.

so i pray, asking You
to listen, as i'm told You do,
as i believe You do,
and as i need You to. to listen,
hearing them,
really hearing them,
and knowing
what to do next
in their world of sores.

abandoned and unloved,
they feel.
bruised and numb,
they are.
acceptance and healing,
they need.

casualties: counting.

scars: deep and ancient
and fresh.
limps: evident
some are, some are
intentionally hidden.
prayers: unknowing
how to request.
but don't You know?
don't You see through
the covers of their exertion
of existence, of survival?

i believe You do.

so, please hear and know
and respond,
now, i pray.

56. what if Jesus came here?

what if Jesus came here
and looked at our faces
and stared into our eyes
and shared our meals
and sang with us
and laughed with us
and cried with us
and entered the
conversations we are
already having?
what would we say?
what do we normally say
that, this time,
His presence might
cause slight reluctance?
what questions would He
ask us?
how would we answer?
would we believe and receive
His love,
feeling no need to perform
or seek to impress?
can we confess,
releasing our lives
to Him,
the One already knowing all?
can we communicate
willingly, honestly,
then with Him?

maybe He's already here
and hearing all.
is that okay?
are we okay

with not being okay
around Him?

i guess He wants us
to embrace Him with us.
the real Him
with the real us,
as we realize
our awareness of reality
can itself, Himself, be the
answer to our prayers.
this time,
His presence,
knowing, hearing,
the truth with Him.

57. when you assume you understand me

the facial expression speaks clearly.
the tone reinforces intent.
the turning away turns the conversation.
the interruption enhances hurt.
the volume returns history.
the moods adjust to the climate.
the forecast changes.
the distance widens.
the potential pleasure becomes pain.
the sentence isn't completed.
the assumptions took its place.
the room doesn't include grace.
the old stories resurrect.
the ancient pain returns.
the escape begins again.
the calm truth wasn't even given a chance.

58. hiring

he defers the privilege,
rejecting an expected response
of *quid pro quo* script.
choosing instead to cherish
honesty, refusing to accept
its disappearance.

desperation appears,
even in a data driven culture,
though often hidden.
investigation intrigues interest
from deeper reasons
for men like him.

he sees through
analysis and trends and
clear components,
processing programs differently.

faces and stories enter
his mind.
fragments and scars
aren't denied.

large puzzles can be best
put together
when all parts are
remembered, found, held,
and put in place.

yes, he will
count the numbers,
calculate the potential,
assess the assessments,

evaluate the value.
yes, he will
match needs with likelihood
of meeting those needs.

but, he will
see through the filtering,
beyond the inputs and outputs.

fortunately, he will
see a person,
a human being,
a life.

and that view,
contrary to common opinion,
can help, not harm,
his decision.

59. not merchandise

depending on a slogan
and leaning on a tag line
we market products through
machines imitating humans
who know us very well
and can always tell
what we prefer.

to create and automate,
to track and detect,
providing venues
for various trends and tricks
to gain a touch
through technology's
chatterbot for bottom line success.
`

displaying deep concerns,
our interests create the turns
we take when results
are all revealed.
the slogans and the phrases,
talking points,
performance, analytics,
the bounce and the brand,
the image on a screen,
the holding of a hand.
is this a healthy art?
are we controlling the control?

amid the artificial,
humans all are customers
in our goals of making profit,
holding data in our hands
and anticipations deep in our heads.

what is in our hearts?
but good business can
be good business when
remembering people as people
rather than numbers or machines.
caring can find a place
in today's campaigns
for those willing
to see through sheets,
finding people
alive, real, and of value.

but how?
power off.
conversations on.
trends aside.
eye contact made
and feelings shared
while refusing to
track or maintain data.
people as people
with people
offscreen, untagged,
no slogan in sight.

60. that missing name

i know the person well.
        they speak.
                i nod.
                        we talk.

after the conversation
        my wife
                asks me the question
                        i hate
                        to be asked,
                                the question
                                        she hates
                                                to ask me.
        "who was that?"

                a name is needed,
                        but a name is hidden.
                                locked in the gray region
                        of
                my
        brain,
the missing noun
                                refuses to be found.

        i dislike,
                or i should say,
                        despise the inability
                                to remember.

                        i try tricks:
                                images,
                                connections,
                                rhymes,
                                repetition.

i try prayers:
        dear God, please provide their name.

i try but too often fail.
i read and hear experts
        reminding us leaders are those who remember names,

    repeat names,
        know names,
            state names.

they label it, and
make it sound easy.

            do they know scar tissue?
            do they know health issues
             limiting mental and emotional
             ability and stability?

    one speaker told tales
    of destruction awaiting those
    who cannot call names.

        their words hurt.
        but i understand
        that they don't understand.

            i know their methods
            of memorization.
            they don't know my battles
            of desperation.

they'll continue remembering
and i'll continue trying.

    maybe we can each teach
    one another.

if i recall this conversation.
and if they remember
that those of us who forget
are also important.

61. the scenes of senegal

i fell in love with the places,
seeing grace
on their faces,
in the scenes of senegal.

so many dreams of desiring to visit
them in their world,
daring to inhale and exhale in dakar.
time with our son aaron and his family.
places, people, events, life.
memories, pictures, activities, times.
preparing, packing, finally flying east,
then seeing their smiles,
there, in what is home to them.

entering a lake rivaling the dead sea,
pink water filled with salt;
i wanted to work to stay afloat,
naturally doing what
i'd been trained to do.
my effort caused problems,
complicating a simple task of trust.
in water exceeding forty percent salinity,
i needed to be—not do.
resting and relaxing, i floated.
the water kept me in a safe place
as my eyes glanced at a wife
and a son and
a sky appearing to smile back,
reminding me that nothing
was the something
i needed most to do.
floating without working,
just resting.

music and a meal
as a singer dropped a few lines
in english
to help us feel welcomed.
rocks on the shore of the sea.
water of an unfamiliar ocean,
though still the atlantic.
two grandsons, together with them
in their world, cherishing each instant.
playing percussion with the natives,
smiling in the joy of their rhythm.
monkeys stealing our pizza.
buildings started but never completed.
natives staring but not understanding
our words.
animals seeming at home.

memories from dakar remain in my mind:
overloaded buses,
people selling things in the streets,
on the road,
strawberries and data cards,
sunglasses seeing
trash everywhere, dirty streets
with prayer rugs on the sidewalk.

i, in whatever time zone, wake early.
so, again, that day, i woke.
opening eyes as my family slept,
seeing a dark room,
feeling the warm air,
closing eyes again,
i listened to a man pleading,
praying in a language
i did not know.
his voice's rhythmic repetition
blew like a breeze through

our open windows
as i opened my eyes again,
and silently prayed a few
of my own prayers.
i breathed, inhaling slowly,
aware of dust in the air,
and noticing an aroma.
i'm uninterested in seafood
for breakfast,
or any meal
of my own.
but their selected food,
fresh and waiting,
somewhere, nearby,
but i hoped not
in our kitchen,
reminded me
i was away from home,
from my home.
i stood up from the bed, digesting
the reality of a visit i will
forever cherish
in their home.

a language i could hear and adore,
but didn't know.
traffic refusing to follow rules,
but choosing to push through
anyone or anything to get anywhere.
thinking often, even while there, of
my upcoming flight back home
alone.

a son waking me
so we could
watch nba playoffs together,
a former normal event

but now a rarity.
our eyes open, our faces smiling,
we saw the long 3s and
the strong dunks, and
we heard dribbles from superstars,
comments from commentators,
shouts from the crowd.
exhausted, but so awake,
we watched. together.

the football i know as soccer,
the walk on the roof while
carrying one grandson
and clinching the hands of another,
staring around
unfinished places,
amid the beauty of clouds and stars.
the religious ritual of prayers
guided my time as a reminder,
holding grandsons, hearing chatter,
feeling the heat, though not
as hot as expected, in africa.
i prayed there. gazing down,
thinking of the neighbors,
smelling their meals,
en imaginant leurs pensées,
j'ai prié là-bas.

a one-hour drive
to
go
four
miles.
i thought i already knew about traffic.
that evening's wild experience
reeducated me.
enjoying a picnic of

breakfast for dinner,
waffles, scrambled eggs, bacon,
and pancakes
in the car, together, on the street,
beside a restaurant closed for ramadan.

i fell in love with those sights,
the bright lights
and noisy nights,
in the scenes of senegal.

their house, their world:
walking down steps to the ground,
walking up steps to the roof.
loving a view from the top.
must it end?
meals. moods. minds.
holding those two boys.
praying for them, for their parents,
for their world.

aaron the chef, the tour guide,
the driver who knows how to
drive and survive amid the traffic chaos.
riding and waiting and
waiting and waiting.
more traffic. more memories.
waking up hearing the call to prayer and
eating their food and
riding on the back of our son's scooter,
while my hands held his chest tightly and
my mind remembered holding him as a child.
he purchased food in a not-so-appealing-environment
and slowly cooked, like the traffic and the waiting,
my ideal thursday meal.

the trip toward home, to airport in a taxi, stopped,

not knowing each other's language, stopped,
not expecting rage on the road, but enduring,
while blending with a new friend
and trusting aaron's predictions of
time and place. listening to people
pleading to make deals,
wanting me to want their food, while stopped
in traffic as my anxious nerves continued
my ritual of would-i-arrive-in-time-for-my-flight
mental narrative
amid the senegalese sounds.

i arrived at the airport on time.
after enduring security three times,
beside the cops,
their faces staring but
their hearts caring,
i assumed.

i flew home, changing flights in new york,
with iphone resurrection at the airport.

debbie and the others would come in one week.

a wedding ring didn't return home with us,
money didn't, people didn't,
food didn't, places didn't,
but memories did, images did,
smiles did.

i left and left
much there.
i learned and am
learning still.
from those places and their cultures,
from those people and their stories,
from those songs and their faces.

debbie's wedding ring
is still gone.
aaron, amber, beckett, and reese
are, again, far from where i type these words.
but we remember, and we sometimes feel
like we still hear the early morning prayers
and float in the saltwater. together.

i couldn't take pink water through customs
on the return home.
but i continue trying—and i
invite you to join me—to let
the salt's reminder become
a custom
to be still
and to schedule
the wonder of nothingness
in our always-too-packed-agendas.

> i fell in love with those days,
> learning the ways
> true care stays,
> in the scenes of senegal.

62. symptoms

sudden and harsh responses,
or no replies at all.

invalid validation
in various forms:
tone of voice,
facial expressions,
direction, if any, of the eyes.

repetition, reservation, characterization,
manipulation, altercation, stimulation.

questions evident but absent.
feelings strong or numb.

a picture-perfect face,
lying to all.

a well-rehearsed fictional script
through stories told on time,
in sequence,
this is evidence;
it is all there.

63. away

he sings his songs revealing
all the questions on his mind,
repetition in a chorus,
when life's not very kind.
words from notes well taken,
then played in notes on key,
from heart and mind all shaken,
seeking to be free.

with his voice up to the mic,
singing it away,
with his hands on the guitar,
playing it away,
together with his band
and the crowd on hand
the songs offered a way
to let the pain,
to let the pain away.

singing from the border,
singing deep within,
singing about a Savior,
singing about a sin,
singing for the people,
singing for himself,
singing for a miracle,
to appear right off the shelf.

with his voice up to the mic,
singing it away,
with his hands on the guitar,
playing it away,
together with his band
and the crowd on hand

the songs offered a way
to let the pain,
to let the pain away.

there surely is a time
when everything he'll sing
can be a type of prayer
releasing wounds to bring
healing his way,
as he sings the pain away,
as he plays the pain away.

maybe it's tonight
when the pain is all released,
and maybe it's tonight
when storms have somehow ceased.
or maybe it's tomorrow,
or sometime very soon.
and maybe he'll keep singing,
to be set free inside this room.

with his voice up to the mic,
singing it away,
with his hands on the guitar,
playing it away,
together with his band
and the crowd on hand
the songs offered a way
to let the pain,
to let the pain away.

as he sings,
as he plays,
as he prays
the pain away.

64. thirty-nine years apart

mama, you left us
for heaven
thirty-nine years ago, today.
i still miss you
as much as ever.
or more.

your smile.
your laughter.
your encouragement.
your care for others.

our conversations.
our ball games.
our prayers.

i wish
i could
wake again to the
sound and smell of
you cooking breakfast.

i wish
we could
watch a ball game together,
listen to songs together,
laugh together,
pray together,
attend a church service together,
and visit our sons
and their families together.

i wish
you and debbie

could have another
of the conversations
y'all had at the kitchen table.

i wish
you could tell stories
to your great grandchildren.

i wish
you'd been nearby when
our sons grew up,
when i pastored a wonderful congregation,
when i became very sick.

i wish
i could talk to you
about my brain damage.

i wish
we could cry together
or sit together
and say nothing.

i wish
i could read to you
stories and poems
i've written,
and eat dinner
together at bar-h
on thursday.
and enjoy a breakfast
at the roystonian,
choosing to talk
about the braves
and not the falcons.

a few lines from several poems

132 chris maxwell

in my latest book are about you.
no one else knows.
but i do.
you listened well,
loved deeply,
smiled often,
and died too soon,
for me.

i'm looking
at pictures of you,
recalling the healing
your laughter brought to me,
and still brings to me as
i imagine
hearing it again.

i'm looking
at pictures of my family
and my life
that you missed,
as we missed you at
the birthday parties,
the thanksgiving meals,
the christmas celebrations
and gifts and aromas of trees,
the florida sunshine and theme parks
and long lines and hot dogs
and ice cream and afternoon storms,
the waves in the ocean
at daytona and st pete,
the georgia autumn colors,
the snow falling and sticking,
the long walks feeling a breeze,
the rides on a boat
on lake hartwell.

i imagine your face,
as i see it now
as i look at a picture from
so long ago,
watching and cheering
for each son
at each game.
you never saw one game
unless, as some say, but
i don't think i believe, that
you have a view from
your present location
to watch
all things
in all places
at all times.

i'm here, alone,
in a house
in georgia
twenty miles from where
we lived for twelve years
and two miles from where
we lived until you died,
and, here, on the
thirty-nineth anniversary of your passing,
i'm imagining what life
would have been
but wasn't,
what life
would be
but isn't.
and, as you taught me,
i've adjusted, just
wishing all along
you were jogging along
beside me

134 chris maxwell

and us
in this marathon.

but you didn't.
and you aren't.
i pray. and reflect.
and, again, as you taught me,
find a way
to be okay.
and smile.

i'm alone
as i write this,
listening to a song
that reminds me of you,
and i'm,
as always,
wishing you were
here—though i'm glad
you are dwelling in that
land of peace.

i'll see you again
there, sometime, someway,
in that
mysterious world of
health and grace and joy.
health, what you needed.
grace, what you lived.
joy, what you displayed.

today, thirty-nine years apart,
i love you.
thank you
for you.

one day,
our divide
will be destroyed
and i'll hug you again.
until then,
i'll play one more
love song
we would listen to together,
as i stare at one more
picture of your face
of grace.

65. now and not yet

now
and not yet.
contentment while
desiring eternal healing.
limping but believing.
embracing a limp,
a collection of scars,
a mental disability, and
seeing more.
hearing here
amid a wait for the there.
alone and together.
faith beside doubt.
asking, studying, working, listening.
mystery made
and in the making.
all done
and much to do.
everything over
and yet to be.
yet, and not
now.

66. finally

a hope.
enduring the waiting.
prayers. and more prayers while
enduring more waiting.
holding on to the hope.
or being held by it.

then, unexpectedly, an arrival.
a dream shifts
from fiction to reality.
i smile.
and give thanks.

those few sentences expose truth.
but a slow process,
or many times
more slowly than slow.
the lengthy line
from hope-in-heart
to thing-in-hand
lures us toward exhaustion.

we open eyes in the dark and ask,
"did i miss it?"
"was i mistaken in assuming
this was the promise?"
"am i wrong?"
limited vision leaves us muffled.

our now is now.
life's now is
wider in space,
deeper in depth,
longer on clock.

it is a process of
a grin glancing from afar
then disappearing in the clouds
before showing itself again
appearing to not even be
coming this way.
but it is.
slowly.

step by step,
breath by breath,
beat by beat,
a process in tune
with the time zone
of development, not demand,
of harvest, not hurry,
of endurance, not thrill.

marathons make us different
creatures. character redesigned,
rediscovered, artistically crafted.

yes, hope.
the waiting with endurance.
while praying
and holding on.
or being held by the hope.
that arrival,
that dream came.
a smile.
after what seemed so long.
all has come.

67. a brief poem with a very long title

death is waiting
for us all.

68. chad

chad, the rain has
finally stopped.

the sky is clear this morning.
the sun's face speeded my routine
of putting my sunglasses on
as quickly as possible.
i stared above, seeing no clouds
for the first time in two weeks.
i decided to walk,
wishing you were here,
walking with me.

my numb hands, wearing no gloves,
feel the cold air,
my dry skin under extra clothes
feels saturday morning wind gusts,
as wet roads from the rain
remind me to walk cautiously.

but no rain is falling now.

i glanced toward your house,
the place you lived for so long
but not long enough for me,
selfishly, i can think that,
honestly, i can say that.
today is the day i would've
texted you or
called you or
knocked on your door and
asked you to walk with me.

i'm imagining now,
while shivering, but
beginning to warm up,
what it would have been like
to walk with you today.
my thick black cap is
covering my bald head
and i'm wearing a sweatshirt,
and a jacket. i'm thinking
about your shoes as i listen
to the rhythm of
my shoes and my steps.
i want to hear
your shoes and your steps,
your stories of
life and pain and hope.
i want to pray prayers
for you
while with you,
walking and feeling the breeze,
stepping over the leaves
that have fallen and
covered our land.
i want to ask you what has
covered your land,
what wind is blowing
into your life and
how are you responding
to that breeze.

oh, what we could
pray today,
this morning, this walk,
to the Maker of that bright light
staring toward us, reflecting from
the sunglasses you gave me,
as i stare into your face

and you turn away,
afraid of what i might say,
wanting you to talk about what you
want to talk about but don't
want to talk about.
offering your humor when
you crave a deeper conversation
of confessions and
requests and petitions.

yes, i wish you were here.
shivering with me.
walking with me.
talking to me.
listening to me,
and, as i often say,
embracing the silence.
you could, and would, tell me
stories about life on the lake.
knowing where to find the fish,
knowing how to catch the fish,
detail for detail,
none understood by me,
but me loving to hear your
southern accent describing
water and lakes and waves
and fish as told by you.
and serious segments of stories,
transitioning humor to fear
and back again,
to God and pain,
and back again,
this account of you
and the weather
in the water of life.
you and your boat and your God.

eventually, we get there.
in the walk, in the conversation,
we get there.
to reality, the pain,
your story, my story.
to the Maker of stories.
to the Writer of stories.
we get there,
in some way,
and some fashion of
mystery and magic, of
grace and mercy,
northeast georgia air in
a january when we
could be and would be
making new year's resolutions
and enduring through disappointments.

my imaginary story ends
when i pass *centerfield*,
the last place we ate together,
the ice cream i still taste as i remember,
realizing again
you're not there,
you're not here,
walking across the railroad tracks.
you're not part of the percussion
of steps on rocks.
this day you are not with me.
you died
too early for me,
unexpectedly for us all.
we worried about you.
we prayed for you.
we aggressively, sometimes,
pursued the conversations,
we casually, sometimes,

pursued the conversations,
i, and others,
wanted, and still want,
more conversations.
about fish and God and pain
and hope,
more conversations,
i'm wanting
still, as i cross streets
downtown in our small town,
more conversations,
at least one more of them,
as i see one leaf flying
through the air,
dancing with a backdrop
of a blue sky, a bright sun;
she flows like
my imagination and my prayers,
up, down,
slowing, speeding up,
then drifting away,
like you did,
like life does,
as we walk and think and pray,
when the rain has stopped
and the sky is clear,
and i wish you
were here.

your pain, chad,
has finally stopped.

69. awareness of you

do you know you?
that you those around you
know well,
do you know that you?
not personal angles toward
your areas of struggle,
but specific details
of life around you and with you,
do you know that you?

denial allows surface peace
but the light weight never ever
gives itself a stare at reality;
brief glances aren't enough.
for you to know you,
you must ask
the right people
the right questions
and listen to their answers.

it will feel like surgery.
your body will be torn apart.
your emotions will become storms.
your motives will deny and defend.
your life might want to end.
but give yourself time
to review yourself as
revealed by those who love you
and carry no other wish
but to help you help you.
they see you from a better glance
than how you see yourself.

i recall an experience of hearing

this type of conversation
about me,
about a me i didn't know was me.
i was wrong.
they were right.
they told me so.
i listened,
in pain, in fear,
with a desire to depart.
i learned about myself
from them.

no, they'll never know
my side of my struggles.
but now i know
their side of myself.
and, if i allow,
that can help me
be a better me.

no, they'll never know
your side of your struggles.
but you can choose to know
their side of you.
and, if you allow,
that can help you
be a better you.

try it.
hear them.
face reality.
know you.
seek help.
and live better after
knowing you better.

70. temporarily permanent

avoiding the truth
in a feeble attempt
to deny
an addiction is
what it is.

reclining back,
feeling discontent,
closing eyes,
choosing rest.
resisting efforts
to be made,
missing out
on what is best.
leaning physically
in the chair's comfort,
avoiding options,
legs up,
shallow breaths,
thoughts down,
continuing the slow sink
of refusing to
face yourself.

your seat is temporary.
your state is permanent.
unless you choose soon
to emphatically attack
the nonchalant, casual,
seat of being controlled.
seeking help,
chasing hands
to lift you from
your chair

of reclining in denial.
naysaying is saying
self-care isn't valued.

addressing your facts is choosing
you have a choice.

your voice,
the one deep inside,
the one of heart, of soul,
the one of hope, of spirit,
that voice
can choose
to not longer
be used
by denial.

step up from the chair.
stare forward.
reach for a hand.
hold it.
or allow hands to
hold you
and help you
walk away from
your former state.
walk toward
what can be,
if you choose.
ensuing transformation,
now.

71. the miles and the hours

miles between us
hold potential for division.

weeks between conversations
contain power for separation.

but not necessarily.

logistically, geographically,
i'm not able to smell the
food you're eating
at your table for dinner.
i'm not able to feel the
wind blowing your way
as you walk from the
parking lot to your office.
i'm not able to notice the
mood you're revealing
through facial expressions,
tone, eyes.

we are apart.

many miles apart.

we haven't talked
for many weeks.

but, so far away,
you're still nearby.
we're still close.
why? how?

distance of space and time
doesn't equal separation.

150 chris maxwell

togetherness is allowed
no matter miles between
or time apart.

modern technology
offers various methods
of tapping figures on a device
and sending you my words.
nouns and verbs and images
deliver moods and confessions
to you. and you
respond, in techno-dialogue
which offers an option,
not stealing the value of
face-to-face time
but flinging possibilities
our way.
to say those words
in some way,
in any way,
and maintain
the conversations.

still living,
undivided, united,
moving through the miles,
making hours and minutes
important for us, now.

72. slowly. surely.

slowly but surely,
the statement says,
as i'm slowly but
not so surely
sure of where this
thinking goes.
we, often,
rush unnecessarily.
forced hurry
from human
denial and determination
deletes a peaceful process
of the long walk,
of the deep conversation,
of the healing while waiting,
of the possibility of
becoming more sure
in the slow pace.

square one.
last straw.
more clichés
with expected meaning
can actually contain
other meanings
if heard, read, viewed differently.

the same for
slowly but surely,
that overused phrase
stated habitually, automatically,
and often unnecessary.

but it, the slowly and the surely,

can keep a deep declaration.
over time, assurance might come.
in no hurry. a will. a way.
a cliché, but much more, living
with confidence in the long
walk of everything.

73. planting seeds

He told stories. parables,
they are called,
emphasizing one point
at a time
to friend and foes,
to crowds
and their questions,
to audiences
of doubters and debaters,
of lovers and haters,
to people like us.

one time, the Storyteller told
one story, illustrating
God's kingdom,
revealing a man scattering seed
on the ground –
a fitting narrative to His audience.

planting, then waiting,
and more waiting.
waiting while work
he could not do
was occurring
as he slept,
as he woke,
as he ate breakfast
as he ate lunch
as he ate dinner,
as he watched
or worked on other goals,
in the labor of survival,
sweat soaking his skin,
sore muscles from many walks

across farm fields
he could not control,
surrounded by weather
he could not control.

snoring in the dark night.
glancing toward the ground
with hopes of a harvest.
feeling the sun's heat.
shivering on cold nights.
but waiting, after planting,
was his task.
whatever his mood,
whatever his assumptions,
he waited.
seeds sprouted,
seeds grew,
though he did not
know how.

by itself, soil
producing grain.
stalk, head, full kernel.
grain ripe, he rejoiced
and responded,
a sickle: the harvest came.

the work, action, in stages,
while he waited.
his job? scattering seed.

that, Jesus said,
is what the kingdom
is like.

the dedication of planting.
the reality of waiting.

the awareness of not being
in control.
the coming of harvest.
in time.
expected but surprising.
wanted but not guaranteed.
hidden but developing.

so, us?
seeds to plant,
lives to live,
time to wait,
results out of our hands.

harvest will come.

74. what kind of christian are you?

"what kind of christian
are you?"
she asked me,
but i wasn't sure
of the question's meaning.
what kind? type? brand?
tall or short,
baby christian or mature christian,
casual or formal,
traditional or contemporary,
protestant or catholic,
young or old,
loud music or soft music,
mainline or charismatic,
a friendly christian
or a cruel christian?

i asked for meaning;
she clarified.
her reference was
to denominational affiliations.
but i continued, and continue,
thinking of her word in question,
her one word in her question:
kind. what kind
of follower of Christ
do i want to be,
am i commanded to be,
should i be?

a kind one.

a follower of Christ who displays
kindness as a lifestyle.

kindness in attitudes.
kindness in actions.
kindness to those who agree
and to those who disagree.
shouldn't church,
a family of Christ's followers,
display love in
what and how and why
all that is done
is done?

contemplate on a biblical story
from first corinthians chapter 13,
the love chapter.
a larger view of the epistle
reveals church conflict,
improper use of spiritual gifts,
speaking in tongues
as a gift used improperly,
disagreements leading to division.
paul, the author, placed
love at the center of the epistle,
reminding readers what matters.
of the various words
translated for us as love, he wrote
agape — that love of choice,
a decision, demanding or expecting
nothing in return.
we could emphasize
various parts of the chapter
on that love,
so many angles,
so many good and needed angles,
for the original audience
and for us.
but i can't shift my
focus away from one line.

paul confessed
speaking words without love
would be "only a resounding gong
or a clanging cymbal," and
he would be not good at all
without love
even if he had faith to move mountains.
he described love as
patient and kind.
he wrote that love
does not envy or boast.
it isn't proud,
doesn't dishonor others,
isn't self-seeking
or easily angered.
it keeps no record of wrongs,
doesn't delight in evil.
it rejoices with the truth,
always protects,
always trusts,
always hopes,
always perseveres.
love, paul wrote, never fails.

yes, so many good and needed angles,
for the original audience and for us.
but i focus on one line:
love is kind.

Jesus displayed that
kind of love, kindness.
in stories He told,
in love He displayed.
loving God and others
were His two main life goals.
kind love.
accepting the unaccepted,

confronting the religious rule keepers
who were not kind to others,
entering conversation with
a woman at a well,
inviting Himself over to visit
a short man climbing a tree,
receiving a hated tax collector's
invitation to dinner.
Jesus was kind—even kind
enough to firmly confront
the unkind ones.
can't we be kind,
like Jesus?
kindness in everyday life:
what we say,
how we view others,
treating others the way
Jesus would.
living lovingly,
but not a false kindness of fake,
insincere, impure motives,
to impress,
to score points.
but genuine kindness,
doing unto others as
we wish they did unto us,
displaying Jesus
wherever we go
and whatever we do
and whatever we say
and how and why
we say what we say.
paul revealed kindness
in another letter as
what he called
the fruit of the Spirit.
it's one of the ways

God displays Himself
through this kind of people,
His children,
through kindness.

what is keeping us from
displaying genuine kindness?
bitterness, unhealthy self-talk,
comparisons, past hurts?
let us address the issues
and pursue healing.
receiving forgiveness.
offering forgiveness.
accepting kindness.
giving kindness.

my story and your story?
of being loved and loving God
and myself
and yourself.
with kindness as
the kind of love.
remember the point:
love is kind.
what kind of church?
a kind church.
what kind of christian?
a kind one.
what kind of person.
like Jesus,
a kind one.

75. a storm and spiritual formation

thunder interrupted our routine.
the noise engaged responses.
bodies shook. eyes opened.
voices spoke brief phrases about
the surprise, the clamor, the storm.
our dark room allowed the
glitters of lightning
to grab all our attention,
shutting our power off, while
revealing power,
reminding us of weaknesses and strength.

we cannot control things.
we want to control things,
but we cannot.
the storm reminds us. now,
sudden volume.

mad rage,
it felt like.
peaceful power,
it might have been.
out of my ability
to do
anything at all
about it,
it was.

students thought through
their next walk.
some were already soaked from
their last walk.
but the next quest
promised more water

as storms dove in force toward
us weak people, objects
feeling the moisture,
but unable to do anything else.

we can do nothing?
we can slow.
we can slow our thinking
even as we run in the water
on the ground, in the air,
on our clothes, in our hair,
sprinting rapidly,
and slowing ourselves
as reminders of the much
we cannot control.

can we learn from the storm?
can we celebrate in the rain?
can we absorb lessons of moisture
needed, even when not wanted?
can we embrace the solitude
in this segment of a storm?

damp. unsure. but teachable.
receiving an education in moisture.
gaining a degree in thunder.
obtaining experience in lightning.
immersed in moisture.
submerged by douse after douse.
steep, marinate, then rinse.
dipping, dunking, sinking.

life is like days like this,
life is like feelings like these.
shifting, not the weather,
but ourselves.
the change from control

to acceptance.
adjusting. resting.
wet, and wise.
afraid, and at peace.
still, and leaving a room,
venturing into a storm.
external war, yes.
internal peace, yes.
of solitude, listening,
lifting petitions,
interceding, realigning,
voicing praise,
asking questions,
reflective thoughts.

a storm of value.
an experience of perspective.
a prayer of confession.
a transformation of us.

76. camilla mae maxwell

i haven't seen you yet.
my imagination sees you.
my anticipation sees you.
my prayers
include you.
there are three more
months of travel
in the adventure of time
before i hold your soft skin
and see your now-unseen eyes
and carry your tiny body
in my walk through
my house or your house.
what lessons will i learn from you?
what lessons will you learn from me?
what lessons will we learn together?
what lessons will you teach the world?
i plan to pray prayers and tell you stories.
stories about yesterdays and tomorrows,
stories with names and experiences,
stories with joy and peace,
stories about us and the world.
prayers as forms of conversations
with your Creator,
the One our eyes can't see—
though i'll guess you'll see
more than i do until we
train you not to see such images—
the Artist who designed you in
His likeness, and will spend
your lifetime continuing
His crafting of your character
as we watch you
open those beautiful eyes

and learn to communicate
with your parents and
with us about
your needs.
when you are tired, sleep.
when you are hungry, eat.
when you feel alone, let
us hold you and tell you
those stories
and sing those songs
and pray those prayers
again and again
as we love you,
and consider ourselves honored
to be a part of your family.

77. reflections on a friday

how to spend a friday?
today, world encephalitis day,
my events reminded me again
of my past and present,
of encephalitis,
of epilepsy,
of scar tissue,
of short-term memory loss,
of exhaustion and moods
and seizures and medication.
recent pain,
honest questions from
my friends, an
honest conversation with
my neurologist,
resulted in our very early
drive becoming a very long
day, including *eeg* and *mri*.
results were revealed this evening:
no new scar tissue,
but a reminder of results
from the chronic injury
long ago. a disease with
long term effects.
extreme swelling,
sharp wave,
expected because of damage.
information given.
instructions given.
i need to follow
rules i offer to others,
and pause
and rest
and, more often,

just say no.
i am thankful for
family and friends
and doctors
who guide me and
accept me and
remind me to
say no.

78. this me and that me

sitting in my office chair on a saturday,
just me and myself,
a me of faith and a me of doubt,
that normal me
and that brain damaged me,
together, processing images
while staring, silently, at a screen.
the images we both observed
were ours.
we both are scarred.

one of us works through the
severely damaged left temporal lobe
acting and performing as if all is in place,
smiling and offering words
for others.
determination.

the other
one of us works to survive.
fully aware of the feebleness,
the hidden but brutal reality
of memory loss.
desperation.

the screen revealed again
scar tissue.
the brain's damage again
stared back.

both observers looked.
both continued looking
as wounds resided in their place
on the screen.

one me wanted to obtain information
from each image,
from each conclusion,
from each fact,
and find ways to move on,
carrying more courage
like it's a cure for myself
and everyone else
in this scar-filled world.

the other me?
he felt tired.
this has been too much,
and gone on too long.
every word search in the brain,
every attempt to state or write
a complete sentence,
every effort to recall a name,
has worn that me down.
maybe it has worn
both mes down.
maybe that me is the only me
willing to notice reality.

which me would win?

an inspirational optimist
turning obstacles into opportunities?

an exhausted realist
staring at an image on a screen?

which voice would speak,
and repeat,
and reinforce options for the
what next
on a morning when both mes

had felt a nagging pain in that
part of the head
for a week.

over two decades had passed
since i almost died.
this day, i returned there.
why now? why more?
why on every day
and every moment
is epilepsy, though often hidden,
so deeply real?

every relationship is affected,
in some way.
every conversation is affected,
in some way.
every attempt is affected,
in some way.

we exited the file.
we grabbed the disk.
we left the office.
we got the keys.
we started the car.
we drove home,
battling which songs to
select for music to
fit a mood.

we aren't the only ones
facing our results of the
wounds from encephalitis
and the
war of epilepsy.
all around me are,
whether or not

they know,
how much or how little
they know.
they might interpret a facial expression
as a disagreement or a rejection,
they might assume mental frustration
equals emotional and relational conflict,
unable to know the desperation
inside my brain,
seeking to understand,
searching for words fitting
a desired response.
they do not know.

we know, though,
that neither of us fully know
what is always the best
or right way to respond.
and no one else really
knows our war.

we both found other things
to do
that day.
things we both agreed on.

we both found our middle
ground again.
a smile while crying.
helping others while self-aware.
exercising the mind while resting.
looking beyond while fully aware.
this me and that me,
both, seeking balance,
refusing to give up.

79. defeating tendencies

we tend to prefer
hide and seek.
we are adults playing
kids' games, but in real life.
we desperately desire
to discuss a topic
we never mention.
will it bring itself up?
we hope so,
we wait to
notice an appearance,
or generate momentum,
or see it just go away.
we've played dumb,
knowing more than what
we know we know.
we've called out at times;
we got a lot done that day.
our plan to push on
is work.
busy, that drug of choice,
fixes nothing at all.
we've felt alone, ignored,
attempting various methods
of revealing reality of wounds,
raising volume, with energy,
guessing tone will change
when time is right.
or we choose.
to address and discuss,
we choose.
with the right person,
at the best time,
for healthy motives,

we choose.
aware, noticing, facing.
choosing to act,
with counsel
and wisdom,
rather than avoidance
and denial,
or overreacting
with anger.
peaceful endurance.
calm reality.
truth, seen through eyes
of love and grace.

80. shifting mind-set

questions have a way.
they can invade us, invite us, dare us
to investigate who we are and
what we do and why.
healthy, fitting, wise, needed
questions can do that, when
asked correctly.
wanting to pursue a better mind-set.
so, know that.
and, do that.
ask. ask the questions.
see what answers might stare back.
preparing for a shift,
slight or significant,
in your mind-set,
ask the questions.

who is in your circle of close, true friends?
who is mentoring you?
who are you mentoring?
what brings you the most joy?
what hurts, fears, doubts are influencing in your decisions?
what hopes, dreams, goals are involved in your decisions?
what are your true strengths?
what are your weaknesses?
what do those who know you best believe about you?
where do you see yourself five years from now?
ten years?
twenty years?
what are you doing today to prepare for then?
what is Jesus saying to you today?
what are you saying in response to His words?

81. twenty-three years ago

this week,
twenty-three years ago,
my life changed.
i felt like i'd entered
another world, observing
a me
i wasn't,
a me
that others believed
i was.

now i know
that me.
that real me.
the me i wasn't
but now i am.

decades later,
lives later,
worlds later,
i'm still adjusting
to me.

knowing, facing,
learning, working through,
receiving help,
rewiring my thinking,
praying,
i'm still adjusting
to me.

82. so much so suddenly

running, running, running,
racing to or from,
rapidly, aggressively,
unaware of now,
a thought, another thought,
a mood, another mood,
so much so suddenly,
rushing from a something
to another something,
emphatically urgent
but forgetting why,
turning from and toward,
a quick cascade of casualties
unnoticed because
of more hurried thoughts.
unaware of reality,
this reality,
of a word, of a face,
of a choice, of a place,
invisible truth,
unheard conversations,
beside, near.

what is missed?
much, very much.
dialogue, where
stories are told,
stories are heard,
eye to eye,
heart to heart,
a healing of community,
a process of authenticity,
a development of transformation.

slow, please slow.
see, please see.
observe, please observe.

stop the sprint.
sit. be still.
pay attention.
one thing at a time,
only one thing at a time,
here, aware,
refusing to run,
choosing to rest,
fully aware of
now.

83. winter to spring

a sudden shift,
winter waving goodbye,
spring staring eye to eye,
smiling, facial expressions
appearing to indicate
a joyful arrival.

wearing a coat, shivering slightly,
i wasn't sure winter
departed peacefully.

calendars do not control
it all.

84. the greatest

the greatest song or show,
the greatest person we know,
or wish we knew,
the greatest meal or game,
the greatest movie or team,
our greatest memories or
greatest friends or
greatest events we wish to
experience again.
basketball tournaments
to reveal
the greatest.
spring training when each
baseball team feels
their potential
to, this time, be
the greatest.
the greatest gift or weather,
the greatest city or feeling,
the greatest ice cream or shoes.
ranking, grading, comparing,
we decide and declare
the greatest.

the disciples of Jesus
were thinking about
the greatest
in a different way.

not the taste or a temporary award.
they wanted to know about
long-term ranking.
which of them, they asked Jesus,
would be among the

leadership team of heaven?
they desired status, recognition.
so, they asked, seeking to
know their chances.

Jesus called a child forward.
the ignored, the uninvited
and unincluded, Jesus
invited and included.
"here," He said, "unless
you become like little children,
you will never enter
the kingdom of heaven."

"whoever welcomes
one such child in My name
welcomes Me."

did they get the point?
do we get the point?

greatness, amid those not
known or expecting to be known
or seeking to be known.

honor, to the silent,
the small, the hidden,
the afraid.

applause, to the forgotten,
the abandoned, the alone,
the willing.

a child can walk up to Jesus
and be held by His hands.
a religious leader would prefer
to debate the words stated

or the walk taken
or the process
or the day
or the time
or the holiness
of those hands.

not all childlike behavior is good.
we are to put away childish things,
to stop thinking like children,
to no longer be infants,
blown about like waves
by the poor teaching and
the deceitful scheming of others.

but this welcomed method of a
childlike mind-set is good.
it is an example of
kingdom leadership.

have we learned this ourselves?
have we seen this ourselves?

"who, here and now,
is the greatest in the kingdom of heaven?"
Jesus sticks with His same
response, echoing the answer again,
a revelation they didn't expect,
we do not expect.
"unless you change and become
like little children,
you will never
enter the kingdom of heaven,"
He said. He says.
"whoever welcomes one such child
in My name welcomes Me,"
He said. He says.

He was and He is
inviting us to be nobodies,
to live godliness with contentment,
to run to Him in desperation,
to live, embracing being with Him
rather than ranking
how much we do for Him.
ending the political agenda.
ending the pursuit toward
the greatest.
embracing life, the Life,
as a child at play.

85. a fading friendship

we were, i thought, friends.
we are, i think, finding
a new relationship.

without investing time,
returns weaken.

not hostile, just amicable.
not belligerent, but stymied.

i consider possibilities
of what could have been
and what could be.

but, for this, i'll leave it all alone.
no urgency pushes.
the craving does not demand
the action required
to resurrect anticipation,
to reach potential.

i tried to maintain it all myself.
i'll now no longer view
any action as vital.

86. on this path together

an expedition of suffering,
feeling rattled,
while reeling in the years.
wearing out, weakening,
but selecting endurance
as the response of choice.
stymied, slightly, while
holding tightly to a hope
kept deep inside
for the ride.

uttering confessions,
choosing to be attentive
in moments, in realities,
on the obvious, on the invisible.

reaching for hands of help,
refusing isolation,
stating requests for assistance:
that phone call from a distance,
that text into deep,
that in person on time
actual human to human
conversation about stories
of waits and dives
and climbs and wounds.

walking on, forward.
holding on, beside.

fellow sojourners caring
instead of judging.
while carrying a little
of the weight

for each other,
the ride can continue.

87. a walk in north georgia

horses refusing to be distracted
from their dinner.
rabbits choosing to hide,
suddenly appearing again
for evening entertainment.
cows uninterested in
my conversations.
mountains maintaining their places
as the earth continues is cycle
allowing the sun to show its
evening goodbye
looking like a large grin
at a friend.

strangers walked by,
i nodded, they nodded,
unknowing each other's stories.
were they as amazed
as i was at the moments
of majestic peace in the
north georgia mountains?

light faded.
night arrived.

gentle sleep.
calm therapy.
rest needed.

morning appeared:
peacefully, cold, pleasant.

i walked to meet and greet
the air, the animals,

the sun's arrival over
small mountains in the east.
the horses were awake,
enjoying breakfast.
the birds didn't hesitate
to publicly reveal their
joyful melodies,
or their fights among family.

the chickens sounded
their alarms, seeming to assume
i was there to do more than stare
and take pictures and write poems.

the sun's arrival fit.
slowly, gradually,
then here,
like a breath, a smile, a song.

gray clouds, almost blue,
shifting slowly around the sky
as i walked and gazed,
praying and marveling
at the mountains
i could see, and contemplating
on the mountains
of life.
height, weight,
stability, significance.
there, as weather wavers
around them,
they stand.

i realized it was time
for breakfast.

88. a display

here we are in
one state, one city,
one building, one room,
many seats, many stories,
many histories, many roles.

a mixture of positions,
one team.

a body of parts,
one bride.

a variety of musical notes,
one key.

a list of titles,
one family.

unity among diversity,
we sit here together
to hear,
to learn, to laugh,
to connect, to reconnect.

so, we ask You to
guide us to grasp
better, newer, effective
ways of inviting,
welcoming, holding others
together with us
in this adventure of grace,
to let us be an assembly
as one
to inform and inspire,

confess and release,
connecting to many,
mentoring a few,
staying true to You,
creatively revealing
reality, here.

now hear us, please,
and guide our words
to display Your face
to the world.

89. changes

the facial expressions in the meeting
indicate stress.
see their eyes?
hear their swallows?
notice their tapping?
they're assessing goals in
amicable credence,
amid expectations taller
than possible.

a meeting for
counting.
a meeting for
scoring.
a meeting for
ranking.

i can ponder the
potential aftermath
of a normal day,
this time spent
feeling locked inside,
but that noise.
that noise outside,
i hear it.
can i listen,
just for a moment?
can i raise
the value of the often ignored
and shift aside
charts and numbers
just for a moment?

to hear the world

away from numbers?
to smell the fragrance
away from stats?
to taste the fruit
away from performance?

if so, maybe the
energy emerges again.
possibly the entire reason
for being here at all
matters again.

but again, maybe the
view outside
changes me deeply,
revealing the low value
of our highly valued goals.

this glance
could change me
for better, forever.

90. a week of transformation

saturday now.
morning moments of
reading, writing,
praying, processing.
today can i spell the word
"therapy" this way:
poetry?
as time travels,
words join in,
moving, advancing,
then stopping,
to dare us to stare
at now.
and be still.

sunday now.
a morning of memories
rush through a mind,
causing thoughts and
feelings to shift, to turn,
as mental poetry
continues riding
through the air,
uncontrolled and unsure.
images of yesterday's
joy and tension:
historical alerts
of a palm sunday,
of a crowd,
of ourselves and myself,
wondering where
this we and this me
fit in the narrative.
applauding then rejecting?

rejoicing then denying?
like poetry's cadence,
life can provide a mixture
of takes.
but i choose, thinking,
to learn again
from them and me
and then and now,
while words
pummel as a diagnosis
of this sunday,
of our trees,
of our crowds,
of our responses
to today's ride.

monday now.
a day for work,
a day for words.
holy, the day is called.
great, the day is titled.
monday, the day is one
more step in a journey
making this week distinct,
a slow shift from
shambles to peace.
listening, trying to hear.
glancing, hoping to notice.
reaching, desiring to touch.
today, i seek to listen again,
remembering, realizing,
daring myself to visit
ancient stories today
and hear the Teacher
amid the noise of
now, monday.

tuesday now.
this week, a melody merging
unexpected segments
into one story.
temple, you'll be torn down.
religious marketing schemes,
you'll be revealed as
missing the points
you promote.
people, all people,
you'll be loved.
that story of Jesus,
so ancient, so relevant,
so needed today
in my heart and mind,
to redirect my own tendencies
and destroy the making
of my own temples.
oh, may i have ears to hear.
oh, may i have a heart to care.
and, may i enter
the story, hearing walls fall,
seeing the rejected loved, and
noticing the facial expressions
of One walking one day
closer to the cross.

wednesday now.
a week's middle.
a story's center.
holy wednesday, spy wednesday,
a day of waiting, of listening,
of hearing the story ourselves,
of entering the story ourselves,
asking, each of us asking,
"where am i in the narrative?"
the deceitful, the oblivious,

the hidden, the obvious,
the negotiations, the control,
the traditions, the transitions:
all is about to change.
today, conversations and calculations
all while Jesus continued,
and continues
His time among them,
His time among us,
together, with sacrificial care,
telling stories, asking questions,
challenging our misunderstandings
of love and truth.
center, middle, wednesday.
then, there, them.
now, here, us.
where am i?
in the narrative
of today, of time,
of change.

thursday now.
the week continues its
route toward redemption.
but these roads aren't smooth,
nothing is simple
during the complexity of
maundy thursday. a covenant
great and holy on
a thursday of mysteries:
moving closer toward a cross,
meals and conversations,
foot washing,
the last supper.
valiant stages,
gentle strength,
pure compassion.

the Leader serves and sacrifices,
setting the plot for tomorrow
on today
as i imagine Him glancing
my way.
He doesn't say anything,
but His eyes do,
and His silence leaves me
asking myself again:
where am i,
where are we,
in the story?
He hands the bread
and the drink.
to me. to us.
to remind me
and us
of Himself and His story
of that thursday
on this thursday
now, closer.

friday now.
good friday is the
name given
about a life given
on this day
so many fridays before
this one.
but how am i changed today
because of this day's history?
how can i be changed
through the truth crafted
in Christ's crucifixion?
i know i don't
fully understand everything,
but i do know

what i can do today,
what i should do today.
i can, and i should, remember.
His pain.
His blood.
His death.
the reason.
the others in the story.
my role in the story.
imagining myself there,
considering all the components
of denial and betrayal,
of sacrifice and death,
of a cross, of a prayer,
of Jesus there for me.
remembering. a realization.
contemplating. a story
redirecting my story
on today's friday.
now, good.

saturday now.
i continue contemplating
yesterday, the friday
we call good.
angry rain fell here,
sounding and feeling
like a waterfall
without the beauty.
thunder played percussion,
her music's mood
displaying power, force.
while i reflected, working
on writing assignments,
seeking to finish tasks,
i heard the regular rhythm
refusing to allow me

to forget.
now today, there's some
silence. less noise.
like that long-ago-saturday:
the story of Jesus
incorrectly assumed
completed, while an
impossible chapter emerged.
noise below the surface.
a miracle venturing near.
promises slowly showing up.
a saturday between,
a story twisting,
a storm calming,
a promise climbing up
from a tomb,
for many lives
of people like us, as
His story there is
storming this way
again and again
on the saturday
between days,
between worlds,
between stories,
between us.
the silence, and noise,
of love.
the force, and calming,
of love.
the death, and life,
of love.

sunday now.
sunrise celebrations.
gatherings to rejoice.
musicals, sermons, prayers.

pictures, smiles, meals.
a reason beyond reasoning:
He is risen! He is risen indeed!
but now what?
today, how are our
lives resurrected?
today, what does the
ancient story mean?
today, are we included
in the narrative?
i'll rejoice. i'll be glad.
and today i'll ask again
what i've asked often,
for the Alive One to live
in me.
that should influence
everything. not a few things,
but everything.
let our resurrection celebrations
include prayers requesting
He live and love
everyone everywhere
through us.
celebrate, and serve.
rejoice, and care.
eat well, and share.
remember, and forgive.
may His life be displayed
through weak and wounded
servants like us.
Christ is risen, now proven
by our deeds.

monday again,
though a new monday.
returning to routine
but renewed.

walking normal paths
but with a better view.
remembering the death
and resurrection,
the stories before
and after,
the names in
the narrative
and our names in
the story.
efforts offered for an
awareness of shambles
amid a distinct backdrop
attempting to validate or mislead,
laboring to prove points or guide astray
in the array of surges
toward better sight.
resting can help.
praying can help.
reading can help.
writing can help.
when invested
in memories ancient and near, in events
obvious and inconceivable:
potential steps to take
like the disciples
fishing again,
eating together again,
seeing even when doubting,
enduring the path
toward death.
and that is life.
real, raw, eternal.
peace, waiting,
for all who choose,
however they feel on a monday,
to believe.

91. 560 days

his words told me the number of days
of freedom.
his facial expression and tone of voice
told me more.
time has traveled as he's pursued freedom
from his lifestyle of dependence;
peace has taken the place of escapism
and avoidance.
he can now talk and feel, and deal
with those feelings.
he knows all could return suddenly,
but he humbly prays and confesses with
a hope that tomorrow will add
one more day
in his adventure of healing.

92. the line kept moving

momentum, moving the line.
advancing, each taking a turn.
with confidence, with patience,
measuring statistics,
trusting analytics,
instincts plus data,
an endeavor to enjoy.
responding, adapting, learning,
as fans stare and cheer,
stand and clap,
boo and ridicule,
amid probable outcomes
and turns not calculated;
it is baseball.

bases and bats and balls.
athletes and coaches.
umpires and fans.
hot dogs and hot days.
teams adjust, evolve,
work, and learn.
fans make noise
and pay prices
for more than
watching ground balls
and home runs
and strikeouts
and double plays
but to breathe baseball air,
to hear sounds of a bat,
to smell aromas of centuries
running, sliding, seeking
to be safe.
it is baseball.

hours of preparing merge
with sudden decisions.
much practice, many predictions,
innings of possibilities,
pitches to be cheered
or questioned.
snacks and drinks offered.
money distributed.
deals made as a
game is played.
newscasts are shoved aside,
if only for nine innings.
it is baseball.

dreamers dream here.
they see visions appear
as if someone else takes
their place, performing for,
and with,
amid the noise and air
and motion of a game
slow for our multi-task days,
but perfect for our need
to pause.
an obsession, a thrill,
a toy, a business.
nostalgic leisure with
intense aspiration,
competitive pursuit
of going home,
that place of starting
and seeking to return,
to slide, to score, to achieve,
to be safe.
it is baseball.

swift and slow.
waiting and all-at-once.

shifts to prepare
based on predictions.
calls questioned.
errors made.
double plays end innings.
homers preferred now
over hits and stolen bases.
line drives.
diving catches.
calls debated.
the sound of a catcher's mitt
mastering an art
as his mind
manages a game on the ground.
it is baseball.

and life?
it too is slow.
it also shifts suddenly
amid this merging
of swinging and missing,
disagreeing with calls,
hoping for rain to stop,
practicing one drill repeatedly,
merging confidence and peace,
waiting for a miracle.
we grab bats and prepare
while on deck.
we stand in the box
assuming we've prepared
as best as possible.
we guess. we rest
on our rehearsal
and trust ourselves,
as the ball comes toward us
at an impossible speed.
life. the working and the waiting.

life. the preparation
and the performance.
life. the spectacular plays
and the unforgettable errors.
life. one pitch at a time.
it is baseball.
it is life.
it is us.

93. pedestrians

darkness, the noticeable art
before the sun shifts the
initial mood,
covers everything.

delightful beauty,
barely visible,
is out of our hands.

we are pedestrians,
observing the delicate
cadence of a whisper.

though we frantically try,
we are not in control.

94. tracking us

our location,
our desired entertainment,
our preferences,
our purchases,
our favorites:
yes, they are tracking us.

foods and songs and colors,
sizes and styles and flavors,
miles and lanes and moods.

but, as our destinations
are revealed
and our tendencies
are disclosed
and our clicks
are funneled,
what if the tracking
of our movements
revealed these words
as descriptions
of our character:
love, joy, peace, patience,
kindness, goodness, faithfulness,
gentleness, and self-control?

more than data and surveillance,
these words might be revealing
ourselves willingly,
as service, on track to
make this world a better place.

95. in this place of now

in athens,
the town i've visited
for bookstores and ball games
and meals and movies,
i sat and walked and
stood and prayed
in a hospital, watching life's
conclusion and introduction,
staring as lives
enter and exit.

i imagined sitting on a
front porch with the two
of them together.
my father-in-law,
in a chair beside me,
grinning and laughing,
telling stories again and
eating food again.
and my granddaughter,
her skin soft and tender,
her life knowing none of the
many stories of pain we could
tell her.
if this image was reality,
i'd ask daddy-o to sing to his
great granddaughter millie.

but it isn't and he can't.
he left us, after his struggle to
breathe ended five days
before she arrived in
the same town,
the same hospital,

the same world,
the same family.

a week of goodbye
and hello.
an experience of departure
and arrival.
a story of ending
and beginning.
a reminder of final words
and first glance.

and now, in this place of
time and space,
new stories and old stories
begin their merging.
staring at gentle eyes,
hearing a baby breathing,
feeling a heart beating,
i think of yesterdays
and tomorrows,
cherishing today, and
choosing, at least for now,
to cradle each now,
refusing to ignore
the wonder among us all.

96. early morning

an early morning walk.
thankfulness and appreciation
and wonder.
a rising sun reminding me i
needed sunglasses—my normal companion.
seeing the remains
of a tiny snake
in his failed attempt
to cross the street.
thinking, praying,
listening, noticing.
embracing the now.

by choice or by chance,
delighting each glance
of liturgical rhythm,
in step and in depth
moving forward, ahead,
toward home.

i cherish outcomes i
seek to see
while also refusing to
miss moments:
sounds of feet pounding pavement,
sights of stars fading and sun waving,
sounds of birds and breeze shouting,
sights of two clouds and a diminishing moon.
the noise, the moment, the morning.

the walk as reality and as a reminder.
to depart and return.
to keep moving.
each step matters,

on mornings,
in memories,
of life.

97. adjustments

like a no-look-pass,
adjustments often
need no warnings.
just slight shifts
of expectations.
not to impress.
to achieve.
to score.
to impact.
during this game,
glance right,
pass left,
knowing your teammate
is open and ready
to receive.

98. expected excellence

their expectations
exceed reality,
transitioning moments
into fictional drama.

missing simplistic value,
their ranking
is a deceitful diagnosis
of authentic love.

welcome the raw.

reject the show.

excellence might
exceed expectations
when acceptance covers
the climate in the room.

99. dreaming about a friend

i still remember the dream.

most dreams i barely recall, if at all.

this dream seemed real,
reminding me of my history
with a friend.

playing against each other
in basketball, then
meeting at a gathering,
engaging in conversations
to begin an authentic relationship.

playing ball. the competition,
the defense, the sweat, the dribbles,
the fakes, the dunks on lower goals,
the long shots, the midrange,
the determination, the laughter,
the building of a relationship on court.

transparent conversations
in offices, in cars, on walks,
establishing something so often
missing: friendship.

we listened to the same music.

we read the same books.

he moved away.

he returned for a visit
to spend time with a new me

encephalitis and epilepsy
had crafted.
he still, i assume, accepted
this weaker me, this me
with a struggle to recall names
and find words and control feelings.

we are years apart now.

we are miles apart now.

i don't know what music he's hearing
or what books he's reading.

but in the recent dream i can't forget,
our conversation
and his prayer and our smiles
at his house merged past realities
to present appreciation, and
left me holding tightly
to the value of friends.
true friends.

i'm still dreaming, i guess.
awake and aware,
directing my thoughts,
but dreaming.
dreaming of more people
experiencing friends like him,
and friendships like ours.
dreaming of more meals and smiles,
more prayers and walks,
more silence and songs,
more books to read and discuss,
when dribbling and driving to the basket
is more symbolic; refusing to stop,
pursuing the points of endurance

216 chris maxwell

and changing a score forever.

wishing i could walk and talk
with him today,
i still dream, and remember.

100. stories

they invite our participation.
they convince our hearts.
they intrigue our minds.
they unveil hidden realities.
they swipe strong patterns.
they capture deep wounds.
they wrestle with us.
they feast with us.
they grieve with us.
they sing songs to us.
they serve us.
they reveal conflict to us.
they unwrap gifts for us.
they craft art for us.
they discover truth for us.
they sprint.
they stop.
they sleep.
they enter eagerly.
they remain experientially.
they exit reluctantly.
they kick doors open.
they slam doors shut.
they leave doors locked.
they allow us a glance.
they offer us a taste.
they provide us a smell.
they are strangers.
they are enemies.
they are friends.
they leave.
they linger.
they hide.
they are our appetizers.

they are our meals.
they are our deserts.
they are here.
they are waiting.
they are alive.
they hold our hands on a sandy beach.
they hug our necks in a hospital room.
they heal our hurts at the operating room.
they shout, frightening us.
they laugh, relaxing us.
they glance, inviting us.
they are professors educating us.
they are pastors shepherding us.
they are chefs feeding us.
they bring conflict.
they introduce characters.
they arrive at conclusions.
they are a coach calling time out.
they are a couple stating marriage vows.
they are a loner living all alone.
they tell us why the song was written.
they take us where the snowman melts.
they turn us when the road looks blocked.
they let us hear a baby cry.
they let us hold hands one last time.
they let us wait for the flight to finally land.

conclusion: enduring the adventure

if we embrace a now but stay there,
refusing to advance,
reluctant to attempt,
resistant in evolving,
what have we done?
who have we become?
for me, as revealed in this collection
of poetic questions and prayers
and confessions and dares,
cherishing each moment provides
nourishment for the next moment.
what has been done crafts
who we can become,
but not all about our accomplishments
and achievements.
better, i believe, is that which we hold,
and the One holding us,
to equip us to endure.
as we suffer, we abide.
as we question, we persist.
like a poem with no final line,
we continue, words and words,
tears and tears, wounds and wounds,
bombarded by beauty
within and far away,
beside and in waiting,
our lives of rhythm and rhyme,
raw lines of frantic verses,
open spaces and covered stanzas,
we endure.
with love and hope and prayer,
with the help of others,
we endure.
beginning again, now, this now,

let us glance at the distant island of
our unknown future,
and grin, knowing we will sail to the land,
scarred but deeply healed, and
grateful for the adventure.

about chris maxwell

Chris Maxwell is a husband, father, and grandfather. He is a writer, spiritual life director, international speaker, and a man who loves people. Chris hopes to be a voice of encouragement through words spoken, words written, and a life lived.

Website/Blog: www.chrismaxwell.me

Twitter: @CMaxMan

Instagram: cmaxman

Facebook: Facebook.com/PausewithChrisMaxwell

Email: CMaxMan11@gmail.com

books by chris maxwell

Beggars Can Be Chosen: An Inspirational Journey Through the Invitations of Jesus

Changing My Mind: A Journey of Disability and Joy

Unwrapping His Presence: What We Really Need for Christmas

Pause: The Secret to a Better Life, One Word at a Time

Pause for Moms: Finding Rest in a Too Busy World

Pause for Pastors: Finding Still Waters in the Storm of Ministry

Pause with Jesus: Encountering His Story in Everyday Life

Underwater: When Encephalitis, Brain Injury, and Epilepsy Change Everything

a slow and sudden God: 40 years of wonder